John Bargrave, James Craigie Robertson

**Pope Alexander the seventh and the college of cardinals**

John Bargrave, James Craigie Robertson

**Pope Alexander the seventh and the college of cardinals**

ISBN/EAN: 9783743309296

Manufactured in Europe, USA, Canada, Australia, Japa

Cover: Foto ©ninafisch / pixelio.de

Manufactured and distributed by brebook publishing software (www.brebook.com)

John Bargrave, James Craigie Robertson

**Pope Alexander the seventh and the college of cardinals**

Christina Regina Sueciæ peregr&#772;
Rom&#257; petiens. An&#778; 1655.

I designed this Figure of the Queene my selfe, and had it cutt in Brass at Jnspruck fo[r] me, w[hi]ch hang in my study. D[r] John Bargrave Canon of Christ Church Canterbury. 1662.

# POPE ALEXANDER THE SEVENTH

AND

# THE COLLEGE OF CARDINALS.

BY

JOHN BARGRAVE, D.D.,
CANON OF CANTERBURY [1662–1680]

WITH A CATALOGUE OF DR. BARGRAVE'S MUSEUM.

EDITED BY

JAMES CRAIGIE ROBERTSON, M.A.,
CANON OF CANTERBURY.

PRINTED FOR THE CAMDEN SOCIETY.
M.DCCC.LX.VII.

WESTMINSTER:
PRINTED BY NICHOLS AND SONS,
25, PARLIAMENT STREET.

[NO. XCII.]

# COUNCIL OF THE CAMDEN SOCIETY

## FOR THE YEAR 1866-67.

*President,*

WILLIAM TITE, ESQ. M.P., F.R.S., V.P.S.A.
ARTHUR ASHPITEL, ESQ. F.S.A.
WILLIAM HENRY BLAAUW, ESQ. M.A., F.S.A.
JOHN BRUCE, ESQ. F.S.A. *Director.*
WILLIAM CHAPPELL, ESQ. F.S.A. *Treasurer.*
WILLIAM DURRANT COOPER, ESQ. F.S.A.
JAMES CROSBY, ESQ. F.S.A.
EDWARD FOSS, ESQ. F.S.A.
SAMUEL RAWSON GARDINER, ESQ.
THE REV. LAMBERT B. LARKING, M.A.
JOHN MACLEAN, ESQ. F.S.A.
FREDERIC OUVRY, ESQ. Treas.S.A.
EVELYN PHILIP SHIRLEY, ESQ. M.A., F.S.A.
WILLIAM JOHN THOMS, ESQ. F.S.A. *Secretary.*
HIS EXCELLENCY MONSIEUR SYLVAIN VAN DE WEYER.
SIR THOMAS E. WINNINGTON, BART. M.P.

The COUNCIL of the CAMDEN SOCIETY desire it to be understood that they are not answerable for any opinions or observations that may appear in the Society's publications; the Editors of the several Works being alone responsible for the same.

# CONTENTS.

### I. THE POPE AND THE COLLEGE OF CARDINALS.

| | | | PAGE |
|---|---|---|---|
| Titles, Preliminary Notices, &c. | | | 1 |
| I. | Pope Alexander VII. | | 7 |
| II. | Cardinal Chigi | | 8 |
| III. | — Rospigliosi (Clement IX.) | | 9 |
| IV. | — Carlo de' Medici | | 10 |
| V. | — Capponi | | 11 |
| VI. | — Sandoval | | 13 |
| VII. | — Francesco Barberini | | 14 |
| VII. | — Rossetti | | 17 |
| IX. | — Bernardino Spada | | 21 |
| X. | — Sacchetti | | 24 |
| XI. | — Ginetto | | 26 |
| XII. | — Antonio Barberino | | 28 |
| XIII. | — von Harrach | | 32 |
| XIV. | — Colonna | | 33 |
| XV. | — Palotta | | 34 |
| XVI. | — Brancacci | | 36 |
| XVII. | — Carpegna | | 37 |
| XVIII. | — Filomarini | | 41 |
| XIX. | — Maculano | | 42 |
| XX. | — Gabrielli | | 44 |
| XXI. | — Fachenetti | | 45 |
| XXII. | — Grimaldi | | 46 |
| XXIII | — Giorio | | 48 |
| XXIV. | — de Lugo | | 49 |

## CONTENTS.

| | | | PAGE |
|---|---|---|---|
| XXV. | Cardinal Orsini | | 50 |
| XXVI | — | Mazzarini | 51 |
| XXVII | — | d'Este | 55 |
| XXVIII. | — | Costaguti | 59 |
| XXIX. | — | Donghi | 60 |
| XXX | — | Rondinini | 61 |
| XXXI. | — | Durazzo | 62 |
| XXXII. | — | Franciotti | 63 |
| XXXIII. | — | Astolli | 65 |
| XXXIV. | — | Azzolini | 67 |
| XXXV. | — | Cibò | 71 |
| XXXVI. | — | Sforza | 72 |
| XXXVII. | — | Savelli | 73 |
| XXXVIII. | — | Vidman | 75 |
| XXXIX. | — | de Retz | 76 |
| XL. | — | Homodei | 79 |
| XLI | — | Lomellini | 80 |
| XLII. | — | Corradi | ib. |
| XLIII. | — | Imperiale | ib. |
| XLIV. | — | Borromeo | 82 |
| XLV. | — | Santa Croce | 83 |
| XLVI. | — | Aldobrandini | 84 |
| XLVII. | — | G. B. Spada | ib. |
| XLVIII. | — | Caffarelli | 85 |
| XLIX | — | Albizi | ib. |
| L. | — | Acquaviva | 87 |
| LI. | — | G. C. de' Medici | 88 |
| LII. | — | Odeschalchi (Innocent XI) | 89 |
| LIII. | — | Ludovisi | 91 |
| LIV. | — | Raggi | 92 |
| LV. | — | Maldacchini | 95 |
| LVI. | — | of Hesse | 98 |
| LVII | — | C. Barberini | 99 |
| LVIII. | — | Pio | 101 |
| LIX. | — | Gualtieri | 102 |

|         |                                          | PAGE |
|---------|------------------------------------------|------|
| LX.     | Cardinal Ottobouoni (Alexander VIII.)    | 103  |
| LXI.    | — Bichi                                  | 105  |
| LXII.   | — Melzi                                  | 106  |
| LXIII.  | — De Elci                                | ib.  |
| LXIV.   | — Farnese                                | 107  |
| LXV.    | — di Bagno                               | 109  |
| LXVI.   | — Buonvisi                               | ib.  |
| LXVII.  | — Pallavicino                            | 110  |
| LXVIII. | — Paolucci                               | 111  |

II. CATALOGUE OF DR. BARGRAVE'S MUSEUM ... 113

Index ... 141

# INTRODUCTION.

THE reader of the following pages will readily understand that to annotate them fully would be a work of very considerable labour. For this reason it is that, although Dr. Bargrave's Manuscripts were copied by me as long ago as 1860, and although the publication of them was announced in the Report of the Camden Society for 1861, they have not appeared until now. The task of editing them was continually deferred, in the hope that I should be able to afford time for performing it thoroughly; until at length, in despair of finding at once the necessary leisure and a sufficient command of the necessary materials, I offered either to hand over the transcripts to any other editor whom the Council of the Society might select, or to send them forth with an amount of illustration far short of my original intention. The second of these alternatives was accepted; and, although the book now appears with but little advantage from editorial care, I venture to hope that for its own sake it will not be unwelcome to the members of the Society.

The writer, John Bargrave, was the younger son of John Bargrave, originally of Bridge, near Canterbury, who built the mansion of Bifrons in the adjoining parish of Patrixbourne,[a] and on it commemorated the virtues of his wife (daughter and coheiress of Giles Crouch of London,) by the motto, "DIRUTA ÆDIFICAT UXOR

---

[a] The house was afterwards rebuilt by the Rev. E. Taylor, whose family had purchased it from the Bargraves, and it is now the seat of the Marquess of Conyngham.

CAMD. SOC.                        b

BONA, ÆDIFICATA DIRUIT MALA."[a] The founder of Bifrons was the eldest of six brothers, of whom Isaac Bargrave, Dean of Canterbury, and progenitor of a family which for some generations flourished at Eastry, near Sandwich, was the youngest.[b]

The younger John Bargrave appears to have been born in 1610. He was educated, like his uncle the Dean, at Cambridge, where he became a Fellow of St. Peter's College, under the mastership of Dr. Cosin, afterwards Bishop of Durham; but from this preferment he was ejected in 1643,[c] and the next seventeen years of his life were for the most part spent abroad. He repeatedly tells us that he four times visited Rome and Naples—each time, as he says, making the crater of Vesuvius his "point of reflection," from which he "faced about for England."[d] The first of these visits was in 1646-7, when he was accompanied by his nephew John Raymond (author of a book of travels which will be noticed hereafter)[e] and by another

---

[a] Hasted, History of Kent, iii. 721, folio ed.   [b] Ib.
[c] See the title of his Catalogue, p. 115; and Walker, Sufferings of the Clergy, ii. 152.
[d] P. 121.
[e] In the Gentleman's Magazine for 1836 and 1837 (vols. vi.—viii. New Series), are printed some passages from a Journal kept by Robert Bargrave, son of the Dean, who accompanied the embassy of Sir Thomas Bendysh to Constantinople in 1646. The travellers landed at Leghorn: "Out of my ambition for the language, as also to see my cousens, Mr. John Bargrave,* and Mr. John Raymond, then at Sienna, I put my viaticum in my purse, and all alone adventured thither, which is about 80 miles within the land . . . . At Sienna I spent almost a fortnight's time in the daily divertisements of musick, horsriding, ballone, and others, courting our palates with ye curious fruits and delicate Muscatella wine . . . From Sienna I was kindly accompanied by my coz. Bargrave as far as to Florence, where he spent 5 days with me, directing me to all that is chiefly notable in and about the city—rarities rather to be named ye described—such in number and quality as the whole world can scarce equal, much less exceed." (vi. 604.)

---

* "Since Dr. of Divinity and Canon of Christ Church, Canterbury, 1662."

young gentleman of Kent, Alexander Chapman, whose portrait appears, with those of Bargrave and Raymond, in a miniature oil-painting, executed at Sienna,[a] and preserved in the Canterbury Library.[b] It must have been on this tour that Bargrave fell in with John Evelyn, who, a quarter of a century later, spoke of him as "my old fellow-traveller in Italy;"[c] and he witnessed Masaniello's insurrection at Naples, in July 1647.[d] In the year of Jubilee, 1650, he again went into Italy, as tutor to Philip Lord Stanhope (afterwards second Earl of Chesterfield[e]) and to the son of Sir William Swan, knight, of Hook Place, in the parish of Southfleet, Kent.[f] The time of the third visit to Rome is determined by the mention of Cardinal de Retz as being there after his flight from Paris in 1654, and of Alexander VII.'s election to the papacy (April 1655).[g] The fourth and last visit was in 1659-60; and at Rome Bargrave heard the news of Charles the Second's Restoration.[h]

In addition to the notices of his Italian travels which are scat-

[a] The party "settled themselves for some moneths at Sienna, to get some knowledge and practice in the vulgar tongue." Raymond's Itinerary, 50. See the foregoing note.

[b] See the Catalogue, No. 67. Chapman was probably the son or nephew of Alexander Chapman, D.D., Prebendary of Canterbury and Archdeacon of Stow, who died in 1629, aged 52.

[c] Diary, May 13, 1672 (vol. ii. p. 73, ed. 1852). The editor wrongly supposes the passage to relate to Dean Bargrave, who had died thirty years before.

[d] P. 41.

[e] This young nobleman was born in 1634. His mother, a daughter of Lord Wotton (with whose family Dean Bargrave was connected by marriage), became a widow about the time of his birth, and, having gone into Holland as governess to the Princess of Orange (daughter of Charles I.), there entered into a second marriage. Lord Stanhope succeeded his grandfather as Earl in 1656. Collins's Peerage, ed. Brydges, iii. 422-5.

[f] Bargrave's pupil was created a Baronet in 1666, but the title became extinct on the death of his son in 1712. Hasted, i. 270.

[g] Pp. 33, 49, 65.                                            [h] Pp. 6, 8.

tered throughout the following pages, we find him sojourning at Leyden, where he picked up Lord Stanhope as a pupil;[a] renewing an old acquaintance with Cornelius Jansen, the painter, at Utrecht;[b] buying maps at Paris,[c] and optical instruments at Nuremberg and Augsburg;[d] seeing sights and adding to his collections at La Rochelle, Saumur, and Toulouse;[e] spending "several summers" at Lyons;[f] visiting Vienna;[g] witnessing the coronation of the Emperor Leopold, as King of Bohemia, at Prague, in September, 1656,[h] and the reception of Christina of Sweden into the Roman Communion, at Innspruck, in the following November.[j] He seems in one passage[j] to speak of London as the starting-place on every one of his Roman expeditions; but the only distinct record of his having been in England under the Commonwealth is a detached memorandum, by which we learn that he left London in April, 1658,—most probably for the Continent.[k]

The Restoration appears to have at once brought Bargrave home. On the 2nd of August, 1660, he recovered his fellowship at Cambridge, by authority of a warrant from the Earl of Manchester, chancellor of the University, "who," says Walker, "had also, no question, ejected him;"[l] and in November of the same year he was recommended to the academical authorities, by royal mandate,

[a] P. 11.  [b] P. 132.  [c] P. xix. of Introduction.
[d] Pp. 131, 131—5.  [e] Pp. 127, 131, 135.  [f] P. 30.
[g] P. 133.  [h] P. 33.  [i] Pp. 68—70.  [j] P. 91.
[k] "Memorandum, Apl. 28, 1658.
"In 2 trunks left with my sister Halsey, at Mr. Lockenton's house at the King's Arms in Knightrider's Street, near Old Fish Street,
"In the pockets of my black cloath breeches left in the hair trunke,
[Inter alia] "2 small pieces of gold, and one of silver, of the coronation of the King of Bohemia, when I was present."
[l] Sufferings of the Clergy, ii. 152.

for the degree of D.D.[a]  Although he had probably entered into holy orders before his deprivation,[b] he was at this time only a deacon; for we read of his ordination to the priesthood by Bishop Sanderson, of Lincoln, at Barbican Chapel, London, on the 23rd of December, 1660.[c]

Being thus qualified for preferment in the Church, he was presented by Archbishop Juxon, in the summer of 1661, to one of the six preacherships in Canterbury Cathedral;[d] in September of the same year, to the rectory of Harbledown; and in July, 1662, to the rectory of Pluckley.[e]  In May, 1662, we find him petitioning the Crown for a prebend at Canterbury, which had become vacant by the death of Dr. Paske.[f]  This application, which was backed by the influence

---

[a] Kennet's Register, 309.
[b] The statutes of the college did not require that more than one-fourth of the fellows should be in holy orders. (Report of Cambridge Commission, p. 307.)
[c] Kennet, 324.
[d] Treasurer's Book of the Cathedral, 1660-1. (MS.)
[e] Hasted, iii. 238, 583.
[f] For Paske (who had been archdeacon of London and master of Clare Hall, Cambridge) see Walker, ii. 26, 141. The petition is as follows:—

"To the King's Most Excellent Ma<sup>tie</sup>.

"The humble petition of John Bargrave, D.D.,

"Humbly sheweth,

"That there being a Prebendaries Place in y<sup>e</sup> Cathedrall Church of Canterbury now voyd by y<sup>e</sup> death of Doctor Paske, and yo<sup>r</sup> pet<sup>r</sup> being of knowne loyalty to yo<sup>r</sup> Ma<sup>tie</sup> and a true son' of y<sup>e</sup> Church of England, for w<sup>ch</sup> he hath beene a great sufferer,

"Most humbly prayes that yo<sup>r</sup> Ma<sup>tie</sup> wilbe gratiously pleased to conferr the said Prebendaries place upon him.

"And yo<sup>r</sup> Pet<sup>r</sup> (as in duty bound) shall ever pray, &c.

"This petion<sup>r</sup> is a worthy person & very capable of y<sup>r</sup> Ma<sup>ties</sup> favo<sup>r</sup> in this particular.

GILB. LONDON."

Domestic State Papers, A.D. 1662, vol. lv. No. 99 (Record Office).  See Mrs. Green's Calendar of State Papers, A.D. 1661-2, p. 394.

xiv INTRODUCTION.

of Sheldon, then Bishop of London, proved successful; and on the 26th of September, in the same year, Dr. Bargrave was inducted to the fifth stall, which, at the reconstitution of the Cathedral under Henry VIII., had been occupied by the venerated Nicholas Ridley, and had more lately been held by Isaac Bargrave before his promotion to the deanery.[a]

At the very time of his installation, Bargrave was about to leave England once more, on an expedition of a different character from any that he had yet undertaken, and one which involved no little personal danger.

A petition had been presented to the King in the name of three hundred British subjects, who were captives at Algiers,[b] and entreated that, by a general collection throughout the churches of England, or by some other means, a sum of money might be raised for their redemption from slavery. In consequence of this petition, a fund of 10,000*l.* was collected—apparently from the bishops and clergy

---

[a] Hasted, iv. 610-11.

[b] The petitioners state that while "in severall English merchant shipps lawfully negotiating in and neare unto the streights of Gibraltar (not certified of the breach of peace with Algier)," they had been "by their men of warr surprised and taken; by which meanes wee and our relations are not only totally undone through our loss of goods, but our selves cruelly inslaved under the horrid tiranny of the insulting Turkes." They go on to state the arts by which the Algerines, "com'ing up with our merchants' shipps, soone carry them (such weake antagonists being overpowered by their monstrous multitude), where some perhaps kill'd in the conflict, the survivers, groaning under a woefull and intolerable captivity, make many supplications to rigid death for a passport." They therefore pray that the King, "by a gathering in the churches of England, or by a summe of money to be raised, or by such other way or meanes as to yo$^r$ Ma$^{tie}$ shall seeme most fitt, will be graciously pleased to ransome and sett us att liberty, before it snow on juvenile heads, the major part of us being in the May of our lives, the sun having not as yet aboarded our zeniths; all of us capable and desirous to serve yo$^r$ Ma$^{tie}$ in the most hazzardous employment."—Domestic State Papers, A.D. 1662, vol. li. No. 24. (See Mrs. Green's "Calendar of State Papers," 1661-2, p. 285.)

alone, and under the authority of Convocation;[a] and with this "hierarchical and cathedral money," (as Bargrave calls it[b]), he and John Selleck, Archdeacon of Bath, were commissioned to go to Algiers.[c] Of their expedition—for which the other commissioner

---

[a] In the Acts of the Convocation of 1661 are the following entries:—

"SESSIO XCVII., 4° Aprilis [1663]......habita consideratione de perficiendo computo doctoris Bargrave, licet absen., usque ad primam sessionem prox. futur. post festum Paschæ prox., reverendus pater [Robertus Oxon.] continuavit," &c.—(Gibson, Synod. Angl. 233, ed. Cardwell.)

"SESSIO CIV. 30° Maii......vocato magistro Syllack, eoque requisito ad conficiend. acquietantiam legalem pro pecuniarum summa per eum a doctore Bargrave recept., et ad introducendam eandem hoc in loco, prox. sessione......idem reverendus pater continuavit," &c. (Ib. 234.)

The mention of an account (*compotus*) in these passages suggests a connexion with an earlier entry:—

"SESSIO XCIII., 5° Martii [1662-3] reverendus pater tractatum habuit de et super computo de......dictusque compotus fuit relatus considerationi reverendorum in Christo patrum Humfridi Sarum. et Georgii Asaphen. episcoporum," &c. (Ib. 232.)

It seemed possible that the blank here might represent some word which might be read by the light of what we know as to Bargrave, although Bishop Gibson, not understanding to what the *compotus* related, had been unable to decipher it; and Professor Stubbs, on referring, at my request, to the MS. (which is at Lambeth), found that the blank ought to be filled up with the word *slaves*—the scribe of Convocation having apparently forgotten the Latin equivalent, and Bishop Gibson having very naturally failed to recognize an English word in such a connexion, more especially as he was unfurnished with any key to the subject of the *compotus*.

We find, then, that the accounts of Bargrave and his colleague were examined by Convocation; whence we may fairly infer that the collection was made in obedience to a resolution of that body. And this circumstance, with the language both of Bargrave and of the document copied in the next note, seems to show that the 10,000*l*. (large as the sum was) were raised from the bishops and clergy exclusively.

[b] pp. 137-8.

[c] With a view to this undertaking, the following licence was granted:—

"Right trusty and right welbeloved Cousin and Councell [*sic*] wee greet you well. The Bishops and clergy of this Realme, in compassion of such poore soules as are at present in captivity and durance under Turkish Governours, have designed Ten thousand pounds towards the redemption and freedome of such a number as y*e* summe will emancipate, And have agreed with diverse Goldsmiths for furnishing them with such a quantity of forraigne coyne as amounts to y*e* summe of Ten thousand pounds in y*e* species of this kingdome, which they cannot transport without our particular lycence.

would seem to have been but poorly qualified[a]—some details may be found in the catalogue of Dr. Bargrave's Museum.[b] As the special passport with which the commissioners were furnished[c] bears date ten days before his installation, we may presume that they left England immediately after the performance of this necessary

"Wee, reflecting on y<sup>e</sup> occ'on, doe hereby require you to give order to y<sup>e</sup> com'ers and officers of our Customes to permit any sum'e whithin that of Ten thousand pounds sterling to be transported by Dr. Bargrave and John Selock, clerk, two persons whom y<sup>e</sup> Hierarchy have chosen, as well-affected and experienet persons, to performe this service, so it be in forreigne coyne. And y<sup>t</sup> you free them of all interruptions and charges in this service. And, &c. Given 15th Sept.

"To our right trusty and right welbeloved Cousin and Connecllo<sup>r</sup> Thomas Lord South'ton, O<sup>r</sup> High Tre'r of England."—Domestic State Papers, 1662, Entry Book iii. 89. (See Mrs. Everett Green's "Calendar," p. 488.)

[a] P. 13<sup>q</sup>.

[b] Pp. 137-8. In Bargrave's accounts, as treasurer of the cathedral, 1669, 1670, are the following entries:—

"May 21. To a poore man that had his toung cut out at Argiers . . . . 1 0
 „   22. To a seaman with one arme, one of those I redeemed from Argirs . 1 0"

[c] There is an entry of a "License to Dr. Jo. Bargrave Mr. Jo. Sellecke" to goe out of y<sup>e</sup> Kingdome, being on his Ma<sup>ts</sup> ispeciall Service for y<sup>e</sup> redeeming of English Slaves at Algiers. 16th Sept. 1662.

Then follows this "passe for Dr. Bargrave and Mr. Sellecke."

"Carolus Dei gratiâ Angliæ, &c. Omnibus Regibus, Principibus, Statibus, Rebusp. et quibuscunq. aliis Christiani Orbis Ordinibus, Amicis et Fœderatis N'ris, ad quos præsentes lyteræ pervenerint, Salutem. Cum virtute Fœderis cujusdam inter nos et Regnum Algirense nuper initi, et in Christiani nominis decus et honorem, Reverendos et dilectos Nobis Viros Johannem Bargrave in [Sac. Theologia] Doctorem, et Johannem Sellecke, S. Th. Baccalaur. et Eccl'iæ N'ræ Bathoniensis Archidiaconû, in id deputandos statuerimus, ut sufficienti authoritate muniti Algerim ad redimendos liberandosq. qui inibi ex subditis N'ris captivi detinentur, N'ro nomine profi[ci]scantur, rogandi a nobis sunt cujuscunq. status et conditionis Amici et Fœderati N'ri uti pio huic operi faventes dictos Reverendos viros non solum liberèq. et tutò ire relinq. sinant, quin et ubi res postulaverit, in oris, stationibus, portubusq. suis benignè excipere et tractare, eisdem victu aliisq. quorum opus erit vitæ commodis justo pretio comparandis amicè adesse velint. In quo sciant se nobis gratum perquam et Christiano dignum esse facturos, cujus vicem, ubi occasio tulerit, lubentes rependemus. Dabantur in Palatio N'ro Westmonasteriensi die Mens. Sept. 16<sup>mo</sup> an'o Ch'ti D'ni 1662, regniq. N'ri quarto decimo." (Domestic State Papers, 1662, Entry-book, vol. viii. p. 244; see Mrs. Green's Calendar, pp. 489-90.)

ceremony; and it appears that they were on their voyage homewards in the month of January following.<sup>a</sup>

As to the latter years of Dr. Bargrave's life, I have been able to glean but little information. In July 1663, he was incorporated as D.D. at Oxford. Two years later, at the mature age of fifty-five, he married Frances, daughter of Sir John Wilde, of Dargate, in the parish of Hernehill, near Canterbury, and widow of —— Osborne.<sup>b</sup> In 1676, he resigned the rectory of Pluckley; in 1680, that of Harbledown;<sup>c</sup> and, on the 11th of May in the latter year, he died, at the age of seventy.<sup>d</sup> His body is interred in the north-west transept of Canterbury Cathedral, under a stone with a plain inscription; but, if his testamentary direction, that a chain taken from the legs of a London merchant, whom he had ransomed at Algiers, should be hung over his grave, was ever complied with, the relic has long disappeared.<sup>e</sup>

Notwithstanding the considerable share of Church preferment which Dr. Bargrave had enjoyed, it appears from his will, dated September 5th, 1670, that he was not free from pecuniary difficul-

---

<sup>a</sup> P. 129.

<sup>b</sup> "March 1665. Dr. John Bargrave, prebend of this church, and M<sup>rs</sup> Frances Osborne, widdow, were maried together the 26th day of March, 1665, by lycense, being Easter-day." (Cant. Cathedral Register.) See also Addl. MSS. Brit. Mus. 5507, fol. 22 b. Although there are several Bargrave pedigrees in the Museum, this (by Hasted) is the only one that mentions anything more of our author than his name. For the lady's family, see Hasted, iii. 11.

<sup>c</sup> Hasted, iii. 235, 583.

<sup>d</sup> Walker, ii. 152; Hasted, iv. 611. The Cathedral Register records that, "May 13, 1680, Dr. John Bargrave, one of y<sup>r</sup> worshipfull prebendaries of this church, was buried in woollen. Affidavit brought in May the 14 following, 1680."

<sup>e</sup> "And the chaine that I took from one of the English sclaves leggs that I redeemed from Algeers to be hung on my grave, with some small motto, for a memorandum of me." See p. 137.

CAMD. SOC.          c

ties;[a] nor had these been wholly got over at the time of his death.[b] Among other legacies, he bequeaths to the library of St. Peter's College "two volumes of Matthiolus on Dioscorides, in Italian,—a rare peece, presented formerly by the States of Venice to the King of England's eminent imbassador Sir Henry Wootton."[c] . . . Sanson's

[a] "Thirdly, in regard that I have had of my deere and vertuously loving wife thirteene hundred pounds, and am bound to secure her joynture by the renewing of my lease, and by reason of my debts am not att present able to renew, therefore, if I dye before her, I give her all the profitt and benifitt of my lease of West Court for ever, hoping that shee will have (as shee hath promissed) a consideration for my nephews Isaac and Robert Bargrave, if there be any thing left when my debts are paid, whereof my debt to her selfe is the cheife. Fourthly, I give my deere wife all things in her closett, two rings, jewells, plate, beding, and whatsoever other household stuffe was hers when we marryed, together with that salve and cuppe with two silver plates that I presented her with on her marriage. My other goods to be sold for the paying of my debts. * * * I make my wife executrix."

[Codicil, Apr. 29, 1676.]

"My deere wife promissed me that if shee had any thing to dispose of att her death the Bargraves should have the best share of it."

[b] See below, p. xx.

[c] For a sight of this book (in two parts, Venice, 1604), which is still in the Library of St. Peter's, I am indebted to the Rev. T. S. Woollaston, Fellow of the College. It contains the following inscription:—

"Thomas Bargrave, sonne to Dr. Isaack Bargrave, Deane of Canterbury, possesseth this booke." "Witnesse, ALB. MORTON.

"Il cui Tomaso, veniendo da morire, dava questo libro al suo Bel-fratello il Sign. Cavaliero Henrico Palmer, milite aurato.

"Moriendo il Sign. Cavaliero lui li dava al altro suo fratello, il Sign. Roberto Bargrave, il maiore nato del Decano.

"Il Sigur Roberto moriendo a Smirna in Asia Minore, i due volume son stato comprato da sua vedoua per me

"GIOVANNI BARGRAVE, Dottore in Teologia, 1661.

"E Canonico della Chiesa Cathedrale di Cantuaria, 1662."

Dean Bargrave had been Sir Henry Wootton's chaplain in one of his embassies, and had married his niece, Elizabeth Dering. Sir Henry appointed "my dear grandnephews, Albert Morton, second son to Sir Robert Morton, Knight, and Thomas Bargrave, eldest son to Dr. Bargrave, Dean of Canterbury, husband to my right virtuous and only niece," as joint executors of his will. The translation of Dioscorides, "in the best language of Toscany, whence her Majesty is literally descended," had been bequeathed by Wootton "to our most gracious and virtuous Queen Mary [Henrietta

maps, together with the other volume belonging to it, which cost me five pounds to the author himself, at Paris;" and " an hundred thirty-three sheets of the cutts in print of Trajan's Pillar, together with the small treatise that explaineth them. They cost me four pistolls at Roome, and are now more hard to be gott."

To the Cathedral Library he gives his " cabinet of medals, with the antiquities that stands upon it in my study, as likewise all my other greater medalons that hang upon the shelves, with the other things on the shelves;" " the great octangular round marble table that standeth in my dining-room;" and " all my larger and lesser mapps of Italy, oulde Roome and new, in sheets at large, very fair, together with all the cutts in my trunks of all the antient ruines, the pallaces, statutes, fountaines, the Cardinalls, souldiers, philosophers, &c. of Italy, France, High Germany."[a]

The rest of his books are bequeathed to his nephew Robert Bargrave, " if he be made a schollar, and sent to either Cambridge or Oxford;" but they are " not to be delivered him untill he is either Batchellor of Art or one and twenty yeares of age." There are also legacies to his nephews John and Thomas Raymond; but, by a codicil dated April 29, 1676, it appears that the nephews were then both dead, and the legacies are cancelled.

To Dr. Bargrave's care his uncle the Dean is also indebted for a monument in Canterbury Cathedral,—a portrait painted on copper,

Maria], for a poor token of my thankful devotion for the honour she was once pleased to do my private study with her presence." (Walton, Lives, 107-8, ed. Oxford, 1824.) Perhaps Thomas Bargrave, having become acquainted with the book when acting as executor, may have found an opportunity of buying it in the course of the troubles which followed. But what is the meaning of Morton's attestation?

[a] The maps and some of the " cutts " have disappeared; the table has been removed to the deanery; the other objects are still in the library.

and inclosed in a marble frame, with an inscription in which are the words, " Johannes Bargrave, S. T. D. Cantianus Posterum Expensis Ponendum Curavit, anno Domini MDCLXXIX."[a]

Mrs. Bargrave lived to the year 1686. From her will, dated July 26, 1685, it would seem that her last days were spent in competence, although she goes into very full details as to Dr. Bargrave's having failed to leave her a sum of 200*l.* which had been promised in the marriage-settlement, and of her having since his death spent upwards of 400*l.* in payment of his debts, funeral expenses, &c. She leaves to Robert Bargrave (the Doctor's " other nephew, Isaack Bargrave, being long since dead,") the lease of West Court, on condition of his paying to her executors, within seven months after her decease, the sum of 600*l.*, and of his releasing them from all responsibilities on account of Dr. Bargrave. She bequeaths small gifts to two of her husband's nieces; and, instead of desiring to share his grave, she directs that she may be buried near her father, in the nave of the cathedral.

Although Bargrave, according to Anthony Wood, was supposed to have "had an especial hand in 'An Itinerary containing a Voyage made thro' Italy in 1647 *and* 47, &c., Lond. 1648, 8vo., by John Raymond, gent.,'"[b] no work has yet been published under

---

[a] The words " Posterum Expensis," (which, as there is no mention of the monument in the will, probably mean that Bargrave had ordered it in the last year of his life, and died without paying for it,) savour of the feeling which is largely expressed in Mrs. Bargrave's will. Dart supposes them to mean " for the information of posterity." (Hist. and Antiq. of Canterbury Cathedral, p. 56, where there is an engraving of the monument.)

[b] Fasti Oxonienses, ii. 267. Raymond was Bargrave's nephew; and we know from Robert Bargrave's testimony (see p. x., note), that they travelled together. Sir John Birkenhead, in a letter prefixed to the book, writes to Raymond : "The thing most

INTRODUCTION.         xxi

his name;" and his present appearance as an author—nearly two centuries after his death—is the consequence, not of his having cherished any literary ambition, but of his passion for collecting curiosities and works of art. It would seem that his gatherings of this kind (however slightly we may now think of them) were somewhat famous in his own day; for Evelyn, in recording a visit to his "old fellow-traveller," describes him as a "great virtuoso;"[b] and Bargrave himself evidently took no little pride in them. The Catalogue of these treasures, in addition to any value which it may have as an evidence of the state of knowledge and connoisseurship in the writer's time, (and, among other things, of the degree to which the arts of dealers in antiquities had already advanced in those days,) is curious and amusing on account of the autobiographical passages

---

observable of all your travells is yourselfe, who was able to graspe so much of the world, when 'tis not twice ten years since you came into it;" a sentence which agrees well with the idea that the nominal author may have been largely assisted by an older hand. Occasionally Bargrave repeats passages from the printed book, without any sign of borrowing, as in the account of Milan (Raymond, pp. 241-2; Bargrave, pp. 82-3), the mention of the Barberini Obelisk (Bargr. p. 73; Raym. p. 103), and the account of Sta. Maria della Vittoria at Rome (Bargr. p. 116; Raymond, 105); and in one place (p. 123), he refers to an "Itinerario d'Italia" as his own production, by which it is possible that he may intend to claim Raymond's "Itinerary," or "Mercurio Italico," as the book is styled in the heading of the pages. On the other hand, the subject for which he refers to his Itinerario, as if it contained full information—Vesuvius—is but slightly treated in the published book. On the whole, perhaps the most likely supposition may be that Bargrave kept a journal, which Raymond was allowed to make use of.

[a] It ought, however, to be mentioned that the Rev. H. J. Todd (sometime a minor canon and sub-librarian of Canterbury, afterwards archdeacon of Cleveland), has quoted some passages from the Book of Cardinals in his edition of Milton (vol. i. pp. 24, 65-7; vol. iv. p. 130, seqq. ed. Lond. 1842; see also his "Lives of the Deans of Canterbury," pp. 296-8.) Archdeacon Todd has given, in his Milton, a very bad copy of the engraving of Queen Christina, which we are now able, by means of photography, to reproduce with accuracy from the original (probably an unique impression), in Bargrave's book; see p. 70.

[b] See above, p. xi.

which occur in it, and has therefore been thought worthy of a place in this volume.

The greater part of the following pages, however, is taken up by the account of Alexander VII. and his Cardinals. Bargrave, on his last visit to Italy, bought a set of portraits of these personages, published by J. J. de Rossi, one of a family which for several generations carried on the production and sale of engravings at Rome.[a]

It would seem, from a memorandum inserted in the book,[b] that Bargrave was in the habit of lending it to his friends for their amusement; and with a view to this he wrote on the margin of the prints, and sometimes, also, on the back of them, such notices of the

---

[a] Out of their establishment grew the papal "Calcografia." (See Nagler, Künstler-Lexicon, xiii. 434-5.) The engravings are good, and the portraits have an air of likeness which is in most cases confirmed by Bargrave's testimony (p. 138, &c.). There is a set of these portraits (wanting, however, that of Alexander himself) in the library of the British Museum. The inscriptions are copied exactly (although in many places it would have been easy to amend them) in the headings of the articles as now printed. The same style of engraving is kept up in the illustrations of Guarnacci's continuation of Chacon's Vitæ Pontificum.

[b] " Pray reade, at your leasure, for pass time—
        The Pope.
        His Nephew.
        Capponius, p. 5.
        Franc. Barberinus, p. 7.
        Rossettus, p. 8.
        Anton. Barber. 12.
        Mazarinus, 26.
        D'Estè, 27.
        Astollius, 33.
        Azolinus, 34.
        Maidalchinus, 55.
        Pallavicinus, 66.
        Odeschalchus,
        the Present Pope, 52."

[The last two lines are in darker ink, and apparently of later date than the rest.]

INTRODUCTION.   xxiii

persons represented as he could glean from books, with additions from hearsay, or from his own observation.

The printed materials for such a series of contemporary sketches were probably then more copious than they have been at any other time. In 1650 appeared at Geneva a small volume entitled " La Giusta Statera de' Porporati,"[a] by a writer who styles himself N.N., but whose real name does not appear to be known. From this book the idea of choosing the Court of Rome for a subject, and a good deal of matter, seem to have been taken by Gregorio Leti,[b] a voluminous writer of equivocal reputation,[c] who put forth anonymously

[a] " La Giusta Statera de' Porporati, dove s'intende la vita, la nascita, adherenza, possibiltà, richezze, offitii, le dignità, le cariche di ciascun Cardinale hoggi vivente, & ivi s'intenderà anco le loro virtù, meriti, e demeriti, con l'aggiunta delli penultimi sei Cardinali, promossi da Innocentio X. l'anno 1648.   Ginevra, 1650."

[b] Melzi, in his " Dizionario di Opere anonime e pseudonime," says of this book (which he himself had not seen), that Leti probably borrowed from it, but can hardly have been himself the author, inasmuch as in 1650 he was only twenty, and as he did not go to Geneva until some years later. The second of these reasons is of little weight, for the careless printing of the book, and especially the badness of the punctuation, seem to show that it was not produced under the author's own superintendence. But the argument from Leti's age is stronger if the date—Rome, May 13, 1648—be correct.

[c] For an account of Leti, see Niceron, Mémoires pour servir à l'Histoire des Hommes Illustres de la République des Lettres, t. ii. Paris 1729; and Chauffepied, Dictionnaire Historique, art. Leti. He was born at Milan in 1630, studied under the Jesuits at Cosenza, and in 1644 went to Rome, where an uncle held high ecclesiastical preferment. This uncle, who eventually became Bishop of Acquapendente, repeatedly urged him to enter into the priesthood; but Gregorio declared himself to be " neither for the sword nor for the breviary;" and the uncle, scandalised by his neglect of religious duties, at length said to him, " God grant that you may not one day become a great heretic; but, for my own part, I do not wish to keep you longer in my house." Gregorio abruptly left the old man, and professed the reformed religion at Lausanne, where he married the daughter of a M. Guérin. From 1660 to 1679 he lived at Geneva. He then removed to England, where he was appointed historiographer to Charles II.; but, on account of the displeasure caused by a book of his, " Il Teatro Britannico," he was obliged to leave the country, and in 1682 he settled at Amsterdam, where he died in 1701. His industry was indefatigable. It is said that he always had in hand three works at once, and Chauffepied enumerates nearly one hundred volumes of his publications. " Outre les ouvrages que Leti a

"Il Nipotismo di Roma,"[a] and "Il Cardinalismo di Santa Chiesa.[b]"

These works were severally translated into Latin, English, French, German, and possibly into other languages; but, although Bargrave uses the English version of the Nipotismo[c] and of the Cardinalismo,[d] he makes no use of the translation of the Statera which had appeared in 1653, and had been reprinted in 1660.[e]

Bargrave does not appear to have been acquainted with some

---

reconnus, il en a fait encore quelques autres, qu'il a eu raison de ne pas avouer, puisqu'ils lui sont encore moins d'honneur que plusieurs des précédens." Niceron, 379.

[a] "Il Nipotismo di Roma, o vero Relatione delle Raggioni che muovono i Pontefici all' aggrandimento de' Nipoti. De bene e male che hanno portato alla chiesa doppo Sisto IV. sino al presente. Delle difficoltà che incontrano i Ministri de' prencipi nel trattare con loro, e insieme col rimedio opportuno per liberarsi da tali difficoltà ; e della causa perchè le Famiglie de' Pontefici non sono durate lungo tempo in grandezza."—Amsterdam, Elzevir [the Hague]. There are two parts, separately paged.

[b] In three parts [M.DC.LXVII.] 1668, 18mo. Leti afterwards published "Il Livello Politico, osia la giusta Bilancia, nella quale si pesano tutte le Massime di Roma e attioni de' Cardinali viventi. In Cartellana [Geneva], 1678, 12mo, 4 vols." But this was not known to Bargrave.

[c] "Il Nipotismo di Roma ; or, the History of the Pope's Nephews from the time of Sixtus IV. to the Death of the Last Pope, Alexander VII. In Two Parts. Written originally in Italian, in the Year 1667, and Englished by W. A." London, 1669.

[d] "Il Cardinalismo di Santa Chiesa ; or, the History of the Cardinals of the Roman Church from the time of their first creation to the election of the present Pope, Clement IX., with a full account of his Conclave. In Three Parts. Written in Italian by the Author of the 'Nipotismo di Roma,' and faithfully Englished by G. H. London, 1670." Folio.

[e] "The Scarlet Gown ; or, the History of all the present Cardinals of Rome. Wherein is set forth the Life, Birth, Interest, Possibility, Rich Offices, Dignities, and Charges of every Cardinal now living. Also their Merits, Vertues, and Vices. Together with the Cariage of the Pope and Court of Rome. Written originally in Italian, and Translated into English by H. C[ogan] Gent. London, 1653." The later edition agrees with this as far as the asterisk, but ends—"Carriages of every of the Popes and Court of Rome. Whereunto is added the Life of the present Pope, Alexander the Seventh." In both editions the heading of the pages is—

    The Just Weight    Of the Scarlet Gowns.

other books on the same or kindred subjects, which had lately issued from the press;[a] but, in addition to the Statera, the Nipotismo, and the Cardinalismo, he was able to draw from certain manuscripts, which are mentioned in his Catalogue (Nos. 65, 66),[b] and still exist in the chapter library at Canterbury.

No. 65 contains two supplements to the Statera. Of these, the first has been little used. The second appears to be really, as it professes, made up of passages written by the author of the book, but omitted in the printing. The cues for the insertion of these passages are given; and in one place, at least, it is clear that there had been a clumsy excision, as the passage, which is nonsense in

---

[a] *E. g.* "Conclave nel quale fu eletto Fabio Chigi, detto Alessandro VII. [No place named]] 1664."

"Il Sindicato di Alessandro VII. con il suo Viaggio nell' altro mondo. [No place] 1688." [This was probably not the first edition.]

Herm. Conringius, "Historia Electionis Alexandri VII. Papæ, &c. Helmstadt, 1657."

With respect to an author of another class, Bisaccioni, who is cited (pp. 18-20), for Cardinal Rossetti's negotiation in England, it may be well to quote Dr. Lingard's remarks on some citations from him in Lord Nugent's "Memorials of Hampden" (vol. ii. Append. A., Lond. 1832). "The comparison of [Bisaccioni's] account with the despatches of [Panzani, Conn, and Rossetti], shows that Bisaccioni was as ignorant of their real history as he was of the politics and conduct of parties in England . . . It appears to me plain that Charles had no idea of a re-union between the churches; and that, if Laud ever cherished such a project, he kept it to himself. Panzani never saw him, nor is there anything in the correspondence, except the assertion of Montagu [Bishop of Chichester, and afterwards of Norwich], to make it appear that the archbishop was favourable to it." (Hist. Eng. vii. 376, ed. 5.)

[b] No. 64, an Italian MS., containing "the conclaves or intrigues of the elections of thirteen Popes," is no longer in the Canterbury Library; but, as it related to an earlier time, would probably have been of no use for Bargrave's purpose. Perhaps it may, so far as it reached, have been the same with a book which is in the British Museum: "Conclavi de' Pontefici Romani, quali si sono potuto trovare, fin à questo giorno, 1667. [No place named, but the catalogue suggests Bologna.] This seems to have originally ended with the Conclave of Alexander VII., those of Clement IX. and X. being each paged separately.

CAMD. SOC. *d*

the printed book, becomes intelligible by the introduction of the words from the Supplement.[a]

The other MS. tract (No. 66) is an Italian translation of an "instruction" which a French ambassador, on leaving his post at Rome, is said to have drawn up for the information of his successor. Under the name of "Baly de Valencé" is meant Henri d' Estampes-Valençay, bailli of Valençay, nephew of Cardinal Achille d' Estampes-Valençay, and himself an eminent member of the Order of Malta, who represented Louis XIV. at the Papal Court, from 1652 to 1656. This tract is said to exist in the original French, in the library of the city of Lyons; but, although another MS. in that library speaks of it as having been "published," the word may perhaps be understood to mean nothing more than that it had been circulated in manuscript copies.[b]

These authorities are used by Bargrave with such freedom, that any attempt to note all his variations from them would impose very great labour on the editor, while it would probably result rather in annoyance than in gratification or instruction to the reader. I have not, therefore, endeavoured to do anything beyond roughly collating Bargrave's notices with the original of the Statera and with the

---

[a] See p. 27.

[b] The Catalogue of the Lyons Library, by De Landine (Paris and Lyons, 1812) t. iii. p. 145, notices among the contents of MS. 1224—

(10) "Lettre du Cardinal Sesi, sur l'écrit publié sous le nom de Baly de Valence [sic] Ambassadeur de France à Rome."

(11) "Instruction de M. Baly de Valence [sic] à son successeur à l'embassade de Rome."

I owe the reference to this catalogue to the "Nouvelle Biographie Générale," art. "Etampes-Valençay, Henri d'." The questions arise—Was No. 10 really written by a cardinal? [There was no Sesi among them, but there was a Cardinal Cesi at the time.] What does the writer mean by publié? Does he really intend to throw doubt on the genuineness of the letter ascribed to the ambassador?

English translations of the Nipotismo and Cardinalismo, noting the passages in which he seems to have misunderstood the words with which he was dealing; nor have I thought it necessary to look at the Italian of the Cardinalismo or of the Nipotismo, except in passages where the printed translations failed to satisfy the suspicions which had been raised by Bargrave's version. It will be seen that, although he evidently prided himself on his familiarity with Italian, his knowledge of that language was really very defective.[a]

The reader will observe that the Cardinals are not arranged in the order of their promotion. This was, of course, originally a mistake; but I have felt myself bound to preserve Bargrave's arrangement, on account of the references which he makes from one article to another.[b] In some other respects, however, I have ventured to take slight liberties with the text. Thus, where the paragraphs of an article were evidently written at different times, I have occasionally re-arranged them in the order which it may be presumed that the author himself would have chosen if the whole had been written at once. I have usually substituted his initials for the full signature—"John Bargrave, D.D., Canon of Christ Church, Canterbury,"—which occurs once or oftener in every article; and, after having given in the first six pages an exact specimen of his very arbitrary spelling, I have contented myself, in the remainder of the volume, with reproducing the most remarkable of his variations from common usage, instead of copying every caprice of his pen.

It can hardly be necessary to say that, in editing this book, nothing can be further from my intention than to serve any contro-

---

[a] For a specimen of his Italian composition, see p. xviii. note.

[b] In these references, the abbreviation of *article* is substituted for that of *page*, in order to avoid confusion with the pages of this volume—each article being in the original limited to a single " page," or rather leaf.

versial interest; or that I do not make myself in any way answerable for the correctness of any statements made by Dr. Bargrave, or by the writers from whom he derived his materials.

In sending forth this volume, it is my agreeable duty to express my best thanks to T. G. Faussett, Esq., Auditor of Canterbury Cathedral; J. G. Nichols, Esq.; W. B. Rye, Esq., of the British Museum; and the Rev. Professor Stubbs, Librarian of Lambeth Palace, for the kindness with which they have assisted me in my inquiries. To Mr. Rye (author of the very curious and interesting volume entitled " England as seen by Foreigners ") my most especial acknowledgments are due, for the great benefits which I have derived from his extensive bibliographical knowledge.

J. C. R.

*Precincts, Canterbury,*
*Nov. 27, 1866.*

---

Since this Introduction was sent to the press, Mr. Nichols has favoured me with some information, derived from Dr. Sykes of Doncaster, as to Alexander Cooke, who is mentioned at p. 140. It appears that Cooke was not Vicar of Doncaster, but that he was resident there in 1646 and the following year, when the baptism and burial of " William, son of Mr. Alexander Cooke, clerk," are recorded in the parish register.

Perhaps this Alexander Cooke may have been the son of a person of the same name who held the Vicarage of Leeds from 1615 until his death in 1632, and was noted as a learned man, of Calvinistic opinions, and the author of some oddly-titled works against the Church of Rome (see Wood's Athenæ Oxon., and Dr. Whitaker's Loidis and Elmete, p. 28. His wife was a sister of Archbishop Bramhall). The younger Cooke became Vicar of Chislet, June 23, 1662, and died in 1672 (Hasted's Kent, iii. 632). He also held the Vicarage of Reculver (ib. 640).

[Title written on a fly-leaf.]

The Pope and Colledge or Conclave of Cardinalles, living when I was my fourth and laste time at Rome, wheare I bought them in sheetes, an⁰ 1660.

JOHN BARGRAVE, of Kent, D.D.,

Cañon of Christ Church, Canterbury.

Mon<sup>r</sup> de Juigné on the word *

[On fly-leaf before the engraved title.]

*Cardinal* is as much as to say *Principal*, upon whome others depend. The 2 poles of the world, the North and the South, are called *Cardines Mundi*, the hinges upon which all the world doth moove. The name of Cardinall (saith he) is very ancient in the Church, as is allso theire dignety, though much increased in lenght of time. One readeth in the Concile at Rome held by Sylvester the First, about the yeare of our Lord 320, that there were 7 Cardinal Deacons. Greagorie the Greate maketh mention of a Cardinal Priest which was also a Bishop (*li.* 2, *Epist.* 25); and as for the variety of them, that there is Cardinall Bishops, Cardinal Preists, and Cardinal Deacons; that is taken frō the places or churches, and is transferred to the persons that governe them. And indeed there were in Rome principal Cardinal Churches, wherein was administred baptisme, and he that administred it was caled a Cardinal-Priest. There were alsoe such as were onely deaconries, and those that governed them were Cardinal Deacons. These assembled to elect the Pope, and he being elected, thay were his assessors and his counsellers. And allthough heretofore all the churches had titles, yet afterwards those churches onely eminent w<sup>h</sup> were governed by a Cardinal. (*Baron. An. Martyrologe.*)

Their order began to be in esteeme under Benedict the VIII., about an. D<sup>ni</sup> 1033, Pope the 152 (*vol. lib.* 21. Volphangus Lazius,

---

* Juigné de la Broissinière, *Dictionnaire Théologique*, &c. Paris, 1644. [It need hardly be said that the authority of this writer is not great.]

## THE COLLEGE OF CARDINALS.

l. 2, c. 2, in his Commentaries of the Roman Repub.) Theire powre in choosing the Popes was not untill about 1059, under Nicolas the Second, the 161 Pope. (*Distinct. Can.* "In nomine Domini.")

By the Council of Bazill, Session 21, the number of Cardinals was not to be above 24, and not any nephew of the Pope or of any Cardinal was to be of that number. (*Session* 23.) As to the colour of theire roabs it altered frō time to time, according to the increase of theire honour. Innocent the IV$^{th}$, the 189$^{th}$ Pope, at the Generall Councill at Lions, ordered the Cardinals to weare red hats and purple gownes, to put them in minde that they were to spende theire blood for to mayntayne the Christian religion; and, that they might have the more respect, he order'd that they shold allwayes goe on horse back about the citty. (*Gaguin.* l. 7; *Æmil.* l. 7; *Martin Poulon.*) Theire other ornaments were added by following Popes, especially by Paul 2$^d$. (*Onuphr.*)

Dr. JOHN BARGRAVE, Canon of X$^t$. Church, Canterb. 1662.

---

[The paragraphs which follow are of later date ; and it will be seen that in the last of these there is a repetition of information already given.]

The scutcheon of armes over the right showlder of every Cardinal belongeth to the Pope that made him a Cardinal. That over the left is the Card. owne armes. And this booke hath but 4 Popes' armes; the Eagle and Dragon, Paul the V$^{th}$, of the Famely of Burghese. The Bees, Urban VIII., Barberino. The Turtle-dove, Innocent X., Pamphilio. And Alexander VII., Chisius.

Of the antiquity of this dignety there are many flatterers ; but it is well knowne that Pope Silvester in a councel held at Rome, an° 324, was the first that caled them Cardinals, as hinges upon which the Church militant was to turne. His designwas good. (*Il Carde-lenismo*,\* pp. 66, 67.)

As to theire habits, which are altogether majestick, they have been prescribed them at severall times, by severall Popes, till at laste Innocent the Fourth, an° 1250, ordered them to weare the red cap, in token of theire readiness to spend their blood for the service of Christ, the head of the Church. (*Il Cardelenismo*, p. 76.)

---

\* So mis-spelled in the MS.

[Engraved Title.]

EFFIGIES NOMINA ET COGNOMINA

S. D. N. ALEXANDRI

PAPAE VII.

ET RR. DD. S. R. E. CARDD.

*nunc viventium.*

*Edit. a Jo. Jacobo de Rubeis, Romae ad Templum Pacis, An. D. 1658.
Cum Priuil. S. Pont.*

[At the bottom of the page is written "JOHN BARGRAVE," with a date, which has been partly cut off in binding; and also

"Comprat. Romæ. in foliis. A Jacobo de Rubeis ad Templû Pacis. Per me JOHAN. BARGRAVE, Generosû Anglum Cantianum, S. T. P. Canonicû Cantuariensë."]

[At the bottom of the publisher's Latin dedication to Alexander VII.]

The College of Cardinalls when I was my fourth and laste tyme at Rome, I being then there when King Charles the Second was restored to his three crownes, and to my knowledge to the greate greife of that triple crowne and that college, whoe thought to have binn masters of England, 1660.

Dr. JOHN BARGRAVE, Canon of Christ Church,<br>Canterbury, 1662.

[On the reverse of the leaf.]

The author of the CARDILANISMO DI SANTA CHIESA to the Reader.*

Many will blame me for writing with that freedome of persons of so greate qualety and now living; and not unworthely; yet, I writing nothing but the truth, it would be cruelty even against nature it selfe, and the right of reason and history, if verety should be persecuted. If the good Catholicks will looke impartially upon what I have written, they will finde my ayme is no other than to admonish the Church of Rome of the errors into which the world imagines they are fallen, and ought therefore to commend the pyety of my designe, there being no greater expression of kindness than for one to advertise his friend of a precipice which he sees not him selfe. And although the Cardinalls perhaps will dispise such advertisements as satyrical, yet have theire eminences no reason to be offended, if they be made acquainted with what the world sayth of them, &c. 1670.

Dr. JOHN BARGRAVE, Canon of Christ Church,<br>Canterbury, 1670.

---

* The passage occurs towards the end of the " Address to the Reader," which is not paged either in the original or in the translation.

## I.

### ALEXANDER VII. CHISIUS SENEN. PONTIFEX MAXIMUS.
### CREATUS DIE VII. APRILIS MDCLV.

In the first months of his elevation to the Popedom, he had so taken upon him the profession of an evangelical life that he was wont to season his meat with ashes, to sleep upon a hard couch, to hate riches, glory, and pomp, taking a great pleasure to give audience to embassadors in a chamber full of dead men's sculls, and in the sight of his coffin, which stood there to put him in mind of his death. [I being at Rome when he was elected (Innocent the Tenth dying), and living there some months after, his extraordinary devotion and sanctity of life I found was so much esteemed that the noise of it spread far and near.* (J. B. 1672.)] But so soon as he had called his relations about him he changed his nature. Instead of humility succeeded vanity; his mortification vanished, his hard couch was turned into a soft featherbed, his dead men's sculls into jewels, and his thoughts of death into ambition—filling his empty coffin with money as if he would corrupt death, and purchase life with riches. The embassadors of Princes and the Cardinals, perceiving that all his apparent aversion to his kindred was but juggling and hypocrisy, made it their business to intreat him to change his resolution, in which they knew they pleased him; but one thing hindered it, and that was the oath he had taken before the crucifix, in the beginning of his popedom, not to receive his kindred in Rome. But the Jesuits, who were his confessors, (vide art. 66,)† found out an evasion, which much pleased his Holiness.

[Il Nipotismo, pt. 2, l. 3, p. 56 (T.)]

[Ds. Pt. I. b. iii. pp. 132-3.]

---

\* The French Ambassador says, "Chigi è 'l maggior erudito che habbi hoggi 'l mondo ..... è di costumi santisimi, e riguardevole in ogni conto, se non che troppo si compiace di certi studij adattati piu a giovani sfaccendati ch' àgl' huomini adoperati nell' affari grandi." fol. 46.

† This reference is to the account of Cardinal Pallavicino.

8                THE COLLEGE OF CARDINALS.

They told him that indeed it was a breach of his oath to receive his kindred in Rome; but that he might with a safe conscience go and meet them half a day's journey out of Rome, and so not at all endanger his soul. Which was put in execution, the Pope going out to meet them at Castel Gandolfo, a house of pleasure of the Pope's, and after some short stay there came back to Rome with them in triumph. But this ridiculous evasion became the subject of Rome's laughter and drollery for a great while, pasquins being set up in every street. [I being at Rome, 1659, found his name grown odious. (J. B. 1672.)

[Ib. p. 135.]

This picture, and all the rest following, are extraordinarily like the persons, drawn and cut by excellent hands, I knowing them at my sight, and some by discourse, as well as I know any of my brethren the Canons of Christ Church, Canterbury. (J. B. 1672.)

The picture before the *Nepotismo* is not like the Pope; this is very like him; I being at Rome at his election and coronation, 1655.]

II.

FLAVIUS TIT. S. MARIÆ DE POPULO S. R. E. CARD. CHISIUS, LEGATUS AVENION. SENEN. IX APRILIS, MDCLVII.

Il Nipotismo, pt. 1, l. 3, p. 138.

He deserves neither to be praised nor blamed for anything regards the government of the Church, in which he is little concerned; for, having the title of Padrone, he exerciseth his mastership in taking his pleasure, avoiding all business, he having given himself up to sensual delights. In his uncle's the Pope's last fit of sickness, that he might not be liable to the imputation of ignorance or incapacity, he bestirred himself pretty well, and performed the duties belonging to so important a place as his is. His assiduity and care appeared much, and the embassadors and people of business were pretty well satisfied with the good will he showed, being the apter to bear with the smallness of his sufficiency. But so soon as his uncle the Pope was well, he gave over giving audience, and feigned himself sick, that nobody might trouble him, and he was really so sometimes out of debauchery; he giving his physicians large presents to hide it from his uncle the Pope.

He doth not much care to gather riches, because his father Don Mario, the Pope's elder brother, is much inclined that way; so that the Cardinal Padrone is content with the revenue of his place, which is above 200,000 crowns a-year, which he spends nobly among his comrades and mistresses. He would without doubt enjoy his health better than he doeth if he were temperate, for he is not above 35 years old, and of a sanguine temper; his beard and hair is of the same colour with his uncle's, [which I that wrote this can witness was very black. I knew him and his father above 10 years at Sienna, when I lived there, and, being afterwards at Rome at his uncle's election, and after that at Rome, 1660, I received several courtesies from those of his uncle's and his Court, especially from Monsignor Gioseppe Vannucio, who had formerly been my Italian Master at Sienna, but was now a prelate clothed in purple silk. This character of this Cardinal I heard at Rome before the Nepotismo was printed.—J. B. 1672.] In his legation to Avinion, in [Ib. p. 140.] France, he got himself much reputation, showing himself noble, liberal, and splendid upon all occasions.

## III.

JULIUS TIT. S. SYXTI S. R. E. PRAESB. CARD. ROSPIGLIOSIUS PISTORIEN'. IX. APRILIS, MDCLVII.

Afterwards chosen Pope by the name of Clement IIX.,* created XX. June, anno M.DC.LX.VII. [The History of Cardinals; or, The Cardinalismo, p. 320.]

* This Pope and his successor ought rather to be reckoned IX. and X. respectively.

He made Monsignor Altieri his Maestro di Camera and afterwards Cardinal; a noble Roman, very rich, the last of his family, and 76 years of age, who succeeded this man in the Papal Chair by the name of Clement IX., and now reigneth, 1670.

## IV.

CAROLUS EP'US OSTIEN. SACRI COLLEGII DECANUS, S. R. E. CARD. MEDICES FLOREN. II. DECEMB. MDCXV.

[La Giusta Statera de' Porporati. No. lxi. p. 218.]

This Cardinal is uncle to the Great Duke of Toscany, as also to the Most Christian King of France. He is a Florantine, and is called the Cardinal of Toscanie, and is the Deane (that is, Senior) of the sacred College. He was promoted to the purple or scarlet as being a great prince, and is therefore of great esteem and authority in the Court of Rome, and was the chief author of the election of Innocent X[th], who carrieth himself to this prince most affectionately, obligedly, and in way of gratitude. He is a great enemy to the family of the Barbarini upon divers occasions, especially for putting their uncle Urban VIII[th] in a war against the Great Duke. He is a sig[nr] of neat sentiments, beloved by all, courteous and splendid. He is pleased to have his gusto and recreations. He is high for the House of Austria, and would be flayed alive for the King of Spain. He is of great age, but beareth his years well. He is a great Prince, and so I leave him.

[I have very often seen him, and am sure this picture is very like him. Vide art. 51.* J. B. 1662.]

* The reference is to the account of the younger Medici.

## V.

ALOYSIUS TIT. S. LAUREN. IN LUCINA PRIOR PRE' CARD.
CARD. CAPPONIUS, S. R. E. BIBLOTE. FLORE. XXIII.
NOVEMBRIS MDCVIII.

He is wanting in the book called " The Just Balance of the Cardinals." I, Anno D⁽ⁿⁱ⁾ 1650, living retired at Leyden in Holland, because of the civil wars in England,—(I having been thrust out of my fellowship of St. Peter's College in Cambridge by the Rebels),—the Lady Stanhope, Countess of Chesterfield, living then at the Hague, employed me in the honourable care of conducting my lord her only son, the now Earl of Chesterfield, Philip Lord Stanhope, into Italy; I telling her Honour that I durst not go a second time to Rome (where I had formerly been) without two letters of protection—one to a Cardinal of the French faction, and another to some Cardinal of the Spanish. Which by her Honour's letters to Paris were procured; the one from Paris, from the Queen Mother, her Majesty of England, to this Cardinal Capponius, whom I knew to be a zealot for the French; the other was by her Majesty's letters to her sister the Duchess of Savoy, at Turino in Piedmont in Italy, which we took in our way. From her Highness we had letters to Cardinal Panzirola, whom I knew to be of the Spanish faction (the usual word at Rome). With these two letters of protection I waited upon his Honour to Rome, the now Sir William Swan, baronet, being likewise under my care, and my Lord's fellow traveller.

Being come, by God's blessing, to Rome, we waited with our letters on their two Eminences the two Cardinals. From each of them we had a very civil audience, especially from this Capponius, and I had several real kindnesses from him, and some from Panzirola, then Secretary to Pope Innocent the Tenth, and lived with him on the Quirinal Hill; where he died whilst we were at Rome,

<sup>Desiderato nella Giusta Statera de' Porporati.</sup>

we being at his funeral eight years before this book was printed. (J. B. 1677.)

This Cardinal stood my friend in several difficulties that I had whilst I lived eleven months that year in Rome, by ordering his auditor to assist me upon all occasions; which he really did by his advice—one time especially, about a pair of pocket pistols, which Sir Thomas Peyton had given his son-in-law Sir William Swan, and found in a portmantle under a bed. By their shortness they were prohibited arms, and the slavery of the galleys or death the punishment to have them. By this Cardinal's auditor's advice, so soon as I (being a stranger) knew that they were prohibited, I dismounted the locks, burned the stocks, and threw the barrels into the River Tiber, as our house stood then convenient; and all this before Italian witnesses, which proved to be our only safety against our Jesuitical enemies. *Sit nomen Domini benedictum!*

That Cardinal's auditor upon this occasion told me that there were two gentlemen prisoners at Rome then which were upon trial for their lives, and that within ten days he thought I might see them executed, being accused for several crimes, but nothing could be proved against them but that, being searched, they were found to have *terzeroli* (as their term was), that is, short pistols, in their pockets. And so it fell out that, shortly after, we effectually did see them executed in the Piazza del Ponte S. Angelo; there being a scaffold first set up, and two long poles fastened to it, resting upon four crutches. Then the criminals were brought thither, their hands being pinioned behind them. Then both of them kneeled down on the scaffold, with each of them an executioner by him with great knobby clubs in their hands, with which they knocked down the prisoners at one side of their heads, giving them a blow or two more when they were down, and then stripped them and quartered their bodies, half-dead, as one might see by their motion. Their heads, with the livers and lungs hanging by the wine-pipes, were first hanged upon those poles, and after them all their quarters, with their privities shaved, as their mode of punishment is to shave like-

wise the heads, to make them the more look like slaves. There
those quarters hanged from the morning until night. I hired a
chamber to see the execution out of a window, but went down
amongst the crowd, and asked what those men had done; and it was
answered Nothing, but only that they were found with prohibited
arms about them. "*Mà questa è la giustizia de preti*—But this is
priests' justice. Oh, these priests, they are bloody men!" And so
I left them railing against the government of priests, and thanked
God that we all escaped as we did, without any trouble, although
our landlord, who was a secular priest, did what he could against
me. But we being strangers, and I having done as I did before
Italian witnesses, I was not only excused, but commended, for
which I may thank this Cardinal, upon the accoumpt of our Queen
Mother's letter to him in my lord's behalf and my own. *Sit nomen
Domini benedictum!*
This picture is very like him.

## VI.

BALDHASSAR TIT. S. CRUCIS IN HIERUSALE' S. R. E. PRESB.
CARD. DE SANDOVAL ARCHIEP. TOLETANUS HISPANUS. II.
XBRIS, MDCXV.

This Cardinal is a Spaniard, and was promoted by Paul V. at the La Giusta
instance of the Catholic King, first, Bishop of Sevil; and, after he Statera de'
had the honour of Cardinal, he was sent embassador to Rome, which No. lxii. p.
charge he carried on with great praise of both courts. His embassy 250.
ended, he returned to his own country, where a long time he could
get no audience of his Catholic Majesty, being kept from it by the
then great minister of state the Conde Duca,* whom he cogeled†
one day with the staff he used to walk with to help him in the gout;

---

* Olivarez.  † *i. e.* cudgeled.

in revenge of which the Conde Duca caused to hamstring his coach-horses when he was going in his coach. Sandoval was he that at his first audience discovered the failings of the said Conde Duca, and of the loss of the kingdoms of Catalonia and Portogall and other states, to which he adjoined also some affairs about the Queen;[*] of the truth of all which the King being informed, he banished the Conde Duca from his court, and reduced him to low condition, to live privately in the country.

The King hath this Cardinal in great esteem, as being the most beloved of the crown. He is very old, of good humour,[†] splendid, of great authority, and well beloved. He is great with Innocent the X., with whom he had great friendship when he was his Nuntio in Naples and in Spain. His old age and the length of the journey hindereth his coming to any conclave.

[Though I have been four times at Rome, at a year of jubilee and at a *sede vacante*, yet I never saw him.—J. B. 1662.]

## VII.

FRANCISCUS EP'US PORTUEN. CARD. BARBER. S. R. E. VICE-CANC. AC SUMMISTA ARCHIPRBR. BASIL. S. PETRI FLORE. II. VIIIBRIS. MDCXXIII.

Il Nipotismo, pt. 1, l. 3, p. 88. [87.]

[P. 88.]

Urban VIII., of the family of the Barbarini, succeeded Gregory the XV. in the popedom, anno Domini 1623. Upon his elevation, his kindred flew from Florence to Rome like so many bees (which are the Barbarino's arms), to suck the honey of the Church, which they did excessively. In the blossom of his popedom, he did one of the worthiest actions of his life, in giving a Cardinal's cap to Francesco Barbarino, his eldest nephew, a personage truly

---

[*] The original is " alli detti del quale s'aggiunsero quei della regina," (p. 251), i.e. the queen made representations to the same purpose as Sandoval.

[†] " di buonissimi costumi."

worthy of so great an honour, being endowed with the singular good qualities of an exemplary life and integrity; and in truth, at [P. 90.] the first, his uncle and he did take no small pains in reforming the abuses, as [well] of the clergy and monks as of the Court and temporal administration, with which all embassadors were much pleased. But after five or six years the Pope left the management of the most important affairs to his nephews. Then they thought of nothing but how to grow rich, to make themselves princes, eternise their family, and fill their coffers with treasure; all abbeys and the best benefices were heaped upon them, being given to some of them [P. 91.] yet in their cradles, of that family.

And indeed the authority which Urban gave to Francesco was [P. 99.] not ordinary, for he thought it not enough to give the power except he gave with it the vanity and title of *Padrone* (that is, *Master* and *Lord*), a title never heard of before at Rome. But Urban had nothing in his mouth but the Cardinal Padrone. " Where is the Cardinal Padrone?" " Call the Cardinal Padrone!" " Speak to the Cardinal Padrone!" Nothing was heard of but the Cardinal Padrone, which the embassadors of princes did not like, saying that they had no Padrone but the Pope himself.*

However, their ambition stayed not at this title. They took [P. 101.] exceptions of the quality of *Illustrissimo*, with which hitherto the Cardinals had been content for so many ages. The title of *Excellency* belonging to soveraine princes in Italy, they strove to find out something that should not be inferior to it, and, canvacing† many titles, at length they pitched upon *Eminency*, which the Princes hearing of it, they took upon themselves the title of *Highness*.

[Since his time the title of *Padrone* continueth to the Pope's chief nephew, and the title of *Eminenza* to all the Cardinals. (J. B. 1672.) The picture is very like him.

* It was not an ambassador, but the Duke of Parma, who, on Urban's speaking to him of " the Cardinal Padrone," interrupted him, and said, " Most holy Father, for my part I know no other Padrone than your Holiness." Nipotismo, 101.

† *i.e.* canvassing.

Every foreign nation hath some Cardinal or other to be their peculiar guardian. When I was four several times at Rome, this Cardinal was guardian to the English; and upon his account the Conte Rossetti was sent into England as a gentleman traveller, but privately the Pope's nuncio. (Vide art. 8.) (J. B.)

When I was at Rome with the Earl of Chesterfield, then under my tuition, 1650, at a year of jubilee, this Cardinal (formerly kind to me,) would not admit my Lord or myself to any audience, though in eleven months' time tried several times; and I heard that it was because we had recommendatory letters from our Queen-mother to Cardinal Capponius (art. 5), and another from the Duchess of Savoy to Cardinal Panzirola, and no letters to him, who was the English (I say, *rebels*') protector, and that we visited them before him.*

A proverb in Italy:—" Quod non fecerunt barbari, fecerunt *Barbarini*."† (Vide artt. 12 et 57.)

" *Il Cardinalismo*," p. 143:—

"*E vecchio Barbarino, ed e Decano,
Ma è troppo duro, e saria gran fortuna,
Calcar due volte il soglio Vaticano.*"‡

" Dean Barbarino is an ancient man,
'Tis hard, and would be strange, if e'er he can
Twice get possession of the Vatican."

---

\* The French ambassador speaks of him as unfavourable to France, but distrusted by the Spaniards, " sapendo quanto che sia capriccioso et amico del suo volere," p. 25.

† " When the Barbarines took away from the Church called the Rotonda [*i. e*, the Pantheon] that excellent piece of workmanship of *bronze* (for which we have no name but *bell-metal*) to make that piece of architecture and pillars which adorn the altar in St. Peter's Church, all the people cried in the streets, *Quod non fecerunt Barbari, fecerunt Barbarini;* and they thought they had a great deal of reason to exclaim thus against them, because it was certainly affirmed that the Barbarines had diverted about half the metal to their private use in their palace; and some say that they made racks for their chimneys of it, but I scarce believe it." *Nipotismo*, 94-5.

‡ " Terzetti sopra i Cardinali del Conclave dell' anno 1667," in " Il Sindicato di Alessandro VII.," p. 289. These lines are quoted in connection with a story that on the death of Alexander VII., Francesco Barberini, " observing new rubs in his way, betook himself to his politics, and prevailed to have the Papacy thrown upon Rospigliosi, that is older and more infirm than he, as not despairing but he may outlive him and have a new push with his pretences."

## VIII.

CAROLUS TIT. S. SILVESTRI IN CAPITE S. R. E. PRE' CARD.
ROSSETTUS EP'US FAENTINUS FERRA. XIII. JULIJ
MDCXXXXIII.

Carlo Rossetti is a nobleman of Ferrara, a spritefull young man when he came to Rome, and got himself to be a prelate, being employed in many affairs by the Barberini * (Pope Urban the VIII's nephews). In which he pleased them well, so that by their means he was sent nuntio into Germany, and after that *into England*, to supply with monies and incourage the Irish Catholics to fight for the Catholic faith against the Parliament; and at his return, by Cardinal Francesco Barberini's means, he was promoted to the purple and the Cardinal's cap, being made Bishop of Faënsa, where he is commended for a good man.† He is not rich, yet liberal in his alms. The present Pope, Innocent the $X^{th}$, hath a kindness for him, although he was against his election.‡ He hath many of his relations that are earls and marqueses in Lumbardy. [This man was shewed me at Rome, to take more particular notice of him, because that he had been almost three years in England the Pope's nuntio, incognito, as you may find in the Italian historian mentioned in the margent. "There arrived," saith he, "at London, to reside at the court ‖ as a gentleman traveller, sent by Cardinal Barberino, but effectually he was the Pope's nuntio, by name Charles Rossetti, an earl by birth, who had taken upon him the

[margin: La Giusta Stattera de' Porporati. [No. lvi. p. 238.]]

[margin: Il Conte Bisaccione, Delle Guerre Civili d'Inghilterra, edit. 2ª, 1653, page 17.§]

---
\* "Da Barberino," i.e. as appears afterwards, by *Francesco*, the subject of the preceding article.

† The French Ambassador speaks very highly of him as a bishop, pp. 41-42.

‡ "Ancorche sia dimostrato poco suo affettionato nell' elettione sua." "Albeit he declared himself but little affected to him in his election."—*Cogna*.

§ The references are accommodated, when necessary, to the 4th edition, Venice, 1655.

‖ "Appresso la regina."

CAMD. SOC.                D

church habit of a prelate; who was of a great spirit, active and prudent, able to undertake business of the greatest difficulty. He was valorous of heart, had a learned tongue, was quick in parts; in brief, he was such an one that his fellow could not be found in all the Court of Rome.\* His letters were dated at Rome the 16th of April." [And then my author tells us a secret that we are not to know.] "And because that in England he wore a secular habit, and took upon him no other name but of Conte Rossetti, therefore I will also hide, where I have occasion to mention him, his title of monsignore, and give him only the title of his noble family. Upon his coming to court, and being courteously received, all things went well with the Ro[man] Catholics, and those priests that by law were to be punished with death were only banished. This was the spring time of the Catholic religion in that kingdom, which flourished by the sweet favourable blasts of the Conte Rossetti. Upon this, libels went about that the King and Archbishop (Laud)† were popish, &c.; whereupon the Archbishop advised the King to rid his court of the Roman ministers, and to renew the rigour of the law. The Conte Rossetti hearing of this, would not hide the interesse for which he was at London;‡ but, upon this occasion, being made more vigorous of courage in this time of danger, thought that now an opportunity was given him to captivate the King's soul, and to conduct him to the Catholic faith, upon which he broke his mind to a confidant courtier of theirs, who yet doubted how to effect it. Rossetti having been persuaded by the Queen to write to the Pope for about an 100,000 lb. sterling § to supply the King's necessities, his Holiness his answer was, ' That the Pope was very ready to supply the King so soon as ever he should declare himself a Catholic, the only available means to loosen the chains of the

---

\* " Che un altro simile forse non havrebbe saputo travare la Corte di Roma."
† " Il Conturberi."
‡ " Il Conte Rossetti, a questi avvisi, la dove altri forse havrebbe presa materia di nasconder gli interessi a che si trovava in Londra, fatto più vigoroso d'animo, &c."
§ " Cinquecento mila scudi."

treasury of the Castle of St. Angelo at Rome. But for a King that should turn to the bosom of the Church he would lay hands on that sacred treasury, otherwise shut up and impenetrable,'" &c.

Where one may hear a great many intrigues about the lending [P. 32, 33.] of this money, and how resolutely the King withstood their attempts, and how Rossetti assaulted the two archbishops to return to the Roman faith.* And then we have mention of Rossetti's letter to the P. 34 [33]. King to persuade him to turn Papist. But he, finding His Majesty immovable and firm as a rock that strongly resisteth the fury of storms and tempests, having his faith and religion fixed and fastened to a more sure foundation, this latent nuntio gave over his fruitless design. "Finding (saith my author) that he gave light unto the P. 35 [34]. blind, that he spake to one that was deaf, and, as the proverb hath it, would with water wash a blackamore white," the (latent) nuntio forsook him, and stole out of England (for fear of the Parliament that sented him) by the help of Sig$^r$ Giustiniano, the Venetian imbassador, and at his coming to Rome *fu decorato della porpora Vaticana.*

Though he was forced to be gone, yet the effects of his nuntiature lasted all our civil war, especially among the Irish rebels. To P. 44 [43]. disprove the calumny that was raised upon the King (probably both by Papist and Presbyterians), he used all the means he could to shew that he was a cordial Protestant, as is seen by his money then coined; so in the several speeches that he made at the head of his army. One of them, saith my author, hath this passage: "If I took P. 80 [77]. a wife of another religion, being of the Roman faith, it was with a universal consent. If the Lord Rossetti came to my court, I used him courteously, as a nobleman and a stranger, as it is fit for princes to do; and yet upon only suspicion, and not guilt, of any wrong to England, I sent him away." My author, in another place, speaking P. 124 [117].

---

* The Italian writer says that they would have been willing to join the Roman Church on being assured of an income of 600,000 crowns, "à fine di poter sostenersi con splendore in Roma," p. 32.

of the death of Archbishop Laud on the scaffold, by way of a scoff, saith, " It had been better for him to have turned Catholic, and to have gone to Rome, as he had been advised by the prudent counsel of the Pope's zealous nuntio, Rossetti, now a Cardinal." And, P. 177 [166-7]. speaking of our King's death, he hath this passage: " His death was foretold (so long ago as when he was Prince of Wales) when he was in Spain, where, he going to visit a holy nun who was much esteemed for her sanctity, she foretold him that, if he did not hearken to the inspirations of that light which his guardian angel should instruct him in, he should die a miserable death, and ruin all his progeny. This angel was Cardinal ROSSETTI, who, by his frequent inspirations, not internal, but to the ear and the eye, by the voice and by writings, by his eloquent and angelical suggestions, indeavoured his conversion to the Catholic faith. Cardinal Rossetti an angel in practice, Great Minister of the Pope, and an angel by his office as being a nuntio or messenger—a zealous nuntio—whence it is no marvel if what the holy nun foretold had its effect."

This picture is very like him. (J. B.)

Cardinal Barberino at Rome (vide art. 8), this man, his agent, here, Cardinal Mazarino in France (art. 26), and Gio. Rinuccini, Archbishop of Firmo in Italy, and the Pope's Nuntio in Ireland, were the Popish ecclesiastics that, by the help of the Jesuits, in all probability were the men that ruined the King and kingdom under the new name and cheat of INDEPENDENT, I being told, beyond the sea, by monks and friars, that I might hear mass where I would among the Independents ; that word signifying only independent as to the Church of England, but dependent as to [the] Church of Rome. And so our war was a war of religion, to bring in Popery; and the King was a true MARTYR, that died for his religion, in revenge for the death of the Queen of Scots, his grandmother.]*

* The French ambassador says that Rossetti's residence in England " gli ha fatto conoscer chiaramente che l'eresie e li scandali sono derivati generalmente in quel regno dalla poca

## IX.

BERNARDINUS EP'US PRAENEST. S. R. E. CARD. SPADA BRISICHELE' PRAEF. CONG. INDICIS, ET CONFINIUM. XIX JANUARIJ MDCXXVI.

He is of Brisighella [by which I know not whether the author meaneth Brescia, in the state of Venice, or Brixia among the Alps, in Tiroll, at both which places I have several times been. J. B.]* He is of a mean parentage, his forefathers being but colliers. He got to be a Prelate, and was put upon great employs by Urban the VIIIth, and afterward was sent into France, where he resided some time, and spent the best part of his patrimony; but at his return, Urban made him a Cardinal, he having in that nunciature pleased both parties. He is a person of great parts, and conversant in matters of all business, and an excellent statist. La Giusta Statera de' Porporati. [No. xix. p. 96.]

He was chosen by Urban the VIII. to take up a difference that happened between his Holiness and the Duke of Parma, who was entered into the ecclesiastic state and [had] taken some castles and places there, and intrenched himself at Aquapendente. To observe whose motions Cardinal Antonio, the Pope's nephew, marched to the frontier with 12,000 foot and 4,000 horse. Spada was sent as plenipotentiary to conclude and adjust the difference, which he did, but he was ill rewarded for his pains, for when he had subscribed to the articles of agreement, whereto as mediators were present the Great Duke of Toscany, the Republic of Venice, and the Duke of Modena.† But when Urban saw the Duke of Parma's forces re- Vide Art. xii. [J. B.]

---

cura de' vescovi, e in particolare dalla dissolutt⁰ⁱ del card'le Vineleffio." (f. 41 b.) The last words make no sense, and it is evident that the transcriber did not understand the passage. Perhaps we might read, " dalla dissolutezza del clero Vineleffio "—the last word being as near an approach as such a writer could be expected to make to some derivative of *Wiclif*.

\* Brisighella is a small town on the river Amone, in the province of Ravenna.

† The awkward construction here is imitated from the original.

turned home, his Holiness declared the articles agreed on to be null and invalid, and that Spada had subscribed them without his consent.\* Upon which the Princes of Italy were much discontented; and, hearing† that the Pope was raising soldiers to go against the Duke of Parma, they armed all with the Duke in his defence. And Spada, to take off the blame from himself, published a manifesto, that what he had done he had done by his Holinesses command; and all had compassion for him. And the event proved to his reputation, for the new war going on, and much blood spent, the Pope was forced to make a dishonourable peace, and to give the several Princes satisfaction.

This Cardinal is no friend to the Barbarini, but zealous for the King of France. He hath an notable headpiece, and full of high thoughts; a poet, historian, and politician.‡ His delight is in his study. But he was very unjust and cruel to Sig$^r$ Andrea Casale, of Bologna, a brave soldier, whom he caused to be made a galley-slave and beaten to death, that he might get a good part of his estate.

Supplimento della Statera, a MS. [J. B.]§

Andrea Casale was a nobleman of Bologna, who, going into the wars of Germany, was there taken prisoner by the Turks, and was sold for a slave, and so lived for many years; in which time a large estate fell to him, and this Cardinal, being legate at Bologna, ordered affairs so that he got possession of a good part of the estate. It so fortuned that Andrea Casale got his liberty, and returned to his country, where he was as a stranger, his relations being loght ‖ to

---

\* Vide Art. xxix. [J. B.] † "Vedendo."

‡ The French ambassador says, "Spada è grande per ogni conto, mà la grandezza del corpo è forsi superiore à quella dell' animo ........ V. E. stia ben con esso, et il modo di guadagnarlo è l'essaggeratione del suo merito, che se poi si dice, che si parla delle sue virtù fuori d' Italia, farà miracoli per ricompensarla di tal aviso con suoi servitij." (Foll. 26-7.)

§ This reference seems to be a mistake. The story of Casale is given at considerable length in the printed "Statera," pp. 100-9, from which Bargrave's narrative is abridged; and it is only the latter part, "Mentre ch'el mondo è mondo, &c.," that is taken from the MS. Supplement.

‖ i. e. loth.

part with the estate they had got by his supposed death; and the Cardinal stood by them to maintain what he had got. The poor gentleman had much difficulty to prove himself to be Andrea Casale; but it happened that his nurse was living, that told the several marks and moules which he had about his body, and by other circumstances he was proved to be the true Andrea Casale. Upon which the Cardinal put him into prison, and sent him away to the gallies, where he was beaten to death. Upon which, saith my manuscript *Supplimento*,—" *Mentre ch' el mondo è mondo, &c.*"—" Since the world [Fol. 38.] was the world, there scarce happened such a case as this, none,—no, not in Barbary [is] com[mitted] such injustice."\* Before Andrea was sent to the gallies, Cardinal Spada went to him in prison to see him, and, being come there, asked him whether he were Andrea Casale,—to which he answered Yes; which the Cardinal hearing, he spit in his face, saying in ill language, " Sirrah, you are not he; but I will punish you like a false raschall." To whom Andrea answered, " You are not worthy of that sacred purple that you wear; and I swear by heaven that, when I come to that which is my own,† I will make you repent it." Upon which the poor nobleman was sent to the gallies, and beaten to death. [I was told this story at Rome, much to the Cardinal's disadvantage. (J. B.)

I have seen him often at Rome, and this picture is very like him. (J. B. 1662).

Dr. Gibbs, an English physician at Rome, who in his poems writeth himself Albanus Gibbetius, my worthy acquaintance, and one of the orators at the Sapientia, where I have heard him on several public affairs make learned orations with a graceful pronunciation;—this gentleman, being of this Cardinal Spada's *equità* (as the term is) or retinue, and much in favour with the Cardinal, as being both poetical,—he gave me this insuing hexastichon:—

---
\* " si commette queste ingiustizie."
† " che se uscirò di qui . . . ." " that, if I get out of this place."

DE ANGLIAE REGE NECATO, ET REGNUM * IN REMPUBLICAM VERSO.  EPIGRAMMA
CARDINALIS SPADAE.

*Privatis tantum cervicibus opta secures*
*(O scelus! O monstrum!) regia colla secat!*
*Sciuditur in partes una cum principe regnum,*
*Cui scindi a toto non fuit orbe satis.*
*Infaustis avibus merito Respublica facta est*
*Publica res quando facta securis erat.*

I am no poet; however the sense in English rithme is this:—

OF THE KING OF ENGLAND'S DEATH, AND THE KINGDOM TURNED INTO A REPUBLIC.
AN EPIGRAM OF CARDINAL SPADA'S.

The axe is for the private subjects' necks,
And not for kings. O horrid monstrous sects!
The kingdom with the king in sunder 's cut,
As from the other world the island 's shut.
That Commonwealth with ill birds doth begin,
Where th' axe is made by them a common thing.]

## X.

JULIUS EP'US SABINEN'.    S. R. E. CARD. SACCHETTUS
FLORENT<sup>s</sup> PRAEFECTUS SIGNAT<sup>re</sup>. JUST. XIX JANUARIJ
MDCXXVI.

La Statera de' Porporati. [No. xviii. p. 90.]

This Cardinal was a merchant's son of Florence, of a good family, partner in trade with Urban the VIII. Father, to whom he was of kindred a good many off. He was first made Bishop of Gravina, in the kingdom of Naples, whither he never went, being suddenly sent by Urban nuncio into Spain, where in that imployment he carried himself with great esteem and satisfaction to that crown; and at his return was made Cardinal, and had many favours of bounty heaped on him, and among them, was made Lord Keeper of the Seal,† which he now injoyeth.

* *Sic MS.*        † The office was " La prefettura di signatura di Giusticia."

He is a person of great worth, and the Barbarini without doubt did think verily in the last conclave * to have created him Pope; but they failed in it, by reason that he was excluded by the King of Spain—not but that he was papa[b]l[e] and deserving, but because the Barbarini were for him.† Others say he was excluded because that at a congregational meeting he was for the reception of the Portugall embassador, and was great with Cardinal Mazzarino, who had formerly been a gentleman of his court.‡ He is of an exemplary life, a giver of alms, rich, and pleasant, but not splendid; being a Florentine, he is, as they are, closefisted and sparing.§ The greatest hindrance to him was the Great Duke, because that Urban the VIII. (formerly his subject) had used him so ill,‖ and he doubted Sacchetti might do so too; the Great Duke not caring to have any of his subjects made greater than himself.

He hath two brothers, Mathew and Alexander. Mathew was he that in the *sede vacante* (when there is no Pope), being saluted by the Barbarini with the title of " Your Eminence "¶ (which belongeth only to Cardinals), as intimating that certainly his brother would be Pope, he upon this opened the cellars of his palace, and for joy gave out wine to everybody that would have it; and when they had well drank, they publicly cried it about—*Viva Papa Sacchetti!* " Long live the Pope Sacchetti!" But when he saw Cardinal Pamphilo elected Pope, with the name of Innocent the X[th], this Mathew through a choleric rage grew stark mad, and so continued a fool; and this madness of his brother was another hindrance of his promotion to the triple crown.

[When Pope Innocent was chosen, the Barbarini, the last Pope's nephews, were fain all to fly, Sacchetti advising the Cardinal

---

* i. e. at the vacancy after the death of Urban, A. D. 1644.
† " per esser troppo affettionato obligato e congiunto di essi Barbarini."
‡ Vide art. xxvi. [J. B.]
§ " uomo ritenuto e ristretto."
‖ " havendo trovato il pontefice Barbarino poco à lui giovevole."
¶ " fu da Barberino trattato con titolo d'Ecclesia, tenendo per sicuro Sacchetti Papa."

Antonio* to set up the King of France his arms as his protector, and to fly into France; which course he followed, but all his revenue was sequestered; and was courteously received by the Most Christian King.]

[Statera, p. 96.] Libels were made, whereof one was—that Sacchetti went into the conclave Pope, but came out Cardinal. [I am sure this picture is like him. J. B. 1662.]

## XI.

MARTIUS EP'US ALBANEN. S. R. E. CARD. GINETTUS VELITERNUS, S^mi. D. N. P. VICAR. G'RALIS. 19 JANUARIJ 1626.

[La Statera de' Porporati [No. xxi. p. 112].] He was born at Veletri, of ignoble parents, he being the son of a day labourer. He came to Rome presently after the creation of Urban VIII. Courting several Cardinals, at length he got into the Prelature (that is, into some office in the Court), by the favour of Cardinal Francesco Barbarino † speaking to his uncle the Pope for him, who afterwards much esteemed him, and promoted him to the scarlet, so that he is the Barbarinos' creature, they having inriched him with many benefices, and made him Vicar of the Papacy, which office is for life. They made him likewise Protector of the Carmelites, and he resideth in the Apostolic Pallaso; and, because he was not known to Princes, nor esteemed much, the Barbarini, to illustrate him in the sight of the world, and notify him to others, sent him upon the great legacie of treating about a universal peace in Germany, that the whole Christianity might acknowledge him an instrument‡ of public good. But the effect proved otherwise; for he carried himself simply and foolishly in that imploy, doing nothing that was fit and handsome for the public, but by sordid sparing and thrift he laid up the Pope's large stipend to inrich his family. At his return, the Pope sent one on purpose to meet him

---

\* Vide art. xii. [J. B.]      † Vide art. vii. [J. B.]
‡ " per principale i-tromento."

at Ferrara, with order to stay there as Legate of that city, where he gathered much riches; and when he came to Rome, the Cardinal Capuchin* paid him all the revenues of his Papal Vicarship, of which he had taken care in his absence; he having given all the good offices he could to his relations, to civilize as much as lieth in him their rustic natures.†

His extraordinary avarice hath caused him to be called by an antonomasia *Il Giudeo*, the Jew.

And Pasquin—

> *Ecco che nella giostra entra Ginetto,*
> *Grave d'età ne s[ar]ebbe in vano*
> *Se il consistorio se facesse al Ghetto.*‡
>
> "Ginetto for the popedom like a dog
> Doth wait; nor would he meet with any clog,
> Were but the Consistory a Synagogue."

The Cardinal is not much learned, although he hath taken great pains in his studies. He is papable as to his age, but the Barbarini would not propound him in the Conclave, foreseeing that they could not compass it—the Sacred College now not only looking upon the man they would choose Pope, but also upon his relation. Nobody courteth him nor visite him, but those that have business with him as Vicar General. He is looked upon as forlorne, yet his pretentions to the Papacy causeth him to be as newter to all princes. Yet, although he had been Legate to the Emperor, it is judged that he is no friend to the House of Austria; but, being the Barbarini's creature, that he is inwardly for the French King.§ [Statera, p. 114.]

* Antonio Barberini the elder, a member of the Capuchin order, and brother of Urban VIII.

† It appears from the MS. Supplement, fols. 38-9, that a passage is here left out as to the preferments bestowed on the Cardinal's brother, of whom it is said that " tutti quelli offizij e dignità non hanno potuto ne saputo incivilire la sua rustica natura." In consequence of the awkward manner in which the excision was made, the passage is unintelligible in the printed book.

‡ Terzetti, p. 289 (see above, p. 16). Il Cardinalismo, pt. 2, lib. 2, pp. 144, 145.

§ The French ambassador advises his successor not to trust Ginetto, " non ch' egli sia

[The picture is very like him, and like that in colours which I have several times seen hung up at Veletri, where he was born, and where he hath built a stately palace, with noble gardens and fountains. It was a city of the ancient Volsi, from whence afterwards sprang the noble race of the Octavians. In going and coming to and from Naples I have lodged there with the *procaccio* (or guide) eight nights. J. B. 1662.]

## XII.

ANT. EP'US TUSCUL. CARD. ANTONIUS BARBERINUS S. R. E. CAM. SIG. GRATIAE ET BREVIUM ET S. CONG. DE PROPAG. FIDE PRAEFECT. ARCHPRBR. BAS. S. MARIAE MAI. MAG. FRAN. ELEMOSIN. ROMANUS. XXX. AUG. MDCXXVII.

<small>Il Nipotismo, pt. 1, l. 3, pp. 89 and 105. Vide art. vii.</small>

These two brothers, Francesco and Antonio Barbarinis, nephews to Pope Urban VIII., though elevated to the same dignity, were nevertheless of a different humour, for one made it his business to edify the public by good actions, and the other did nothing but scandalize all the world by his vicious deportments; insomuch that whosoever will weigh the virtues of the one against the vices of the other shall see that the ill actions of Cardinal Antonio are far heavier than the good ones of the brother, though his brother's piety be very great. But when once he began to frequent the French, he changed, as it were, his nature; for of a covetous hater of learning he became a generous promoter of ingenuity, a noble prince, and a good Cardinal. First he led a life full of liberty and debauchery, and made embassadors and the Romans hate him, so that at midnight they would cry in the streets,

<small>[P. 105.]</small>

*Il Cardinal Antonio*
*Serve in Roma di Demonio.*

amico delli Spagnuoli, mà perche è di quella razza di persone che odiano tutti per esser meritevoli dell' abbominattione d' ognuo." (Fol. 286.)

But after that he changed his nature and humour they changed their note, and cried—

*Antonio Barberino*
*Sembra un angelo divino.*

Never prince was more absolute in a conquest than the Barba- [P. 102.]
rinos were in their administration of the Church and City of Rome.
Their uncle being Pope xxiiii. years, in the whole consistory of
Cardinals there were but five who were not their creatures; so they,
having all the rest at their command, lorded it over the Church and
State, and over all Christendom [under their papistical power *], as
monarchs of the world.

[When Urban the VIII. their uncle was dead, the Barbarinos in the
conclave made all the opposition they possibly could against Cardinal
Pamphilio, a creature of their uncle's, and that had been their tutor
in their minority, and a severe man; but, sore against their will, he
was chosen Pope by the name of Innocent the Tenth, under whom
the Barbarinos suffered a sharp persecution of sequestration, and P. 104.
this Antonio of exile. At my first going into Italy, an° 1646,
I, passing over the Alps, met him in a soldierly travelling habit
among the mountains at a small inn, where I had discourse with
him. Some of his retinue told me who he was, how he was banished
Rome, but, before he left it, he had set up the King of France's
arms over his pallace door, as taking him for his protector; and
that he was now going into France, where he was made that King's
great almoner. J. B. 1672.†

I bought his picture on horseback in armour, as he was general
of 20,000 men, in his uncle's wars against the Duke of Tuscany
and Parma, and had several businesses with him. J. B.‡

The author of the " Statera Giusta," I doubt, had been wronged
or offended by him, for he giveth him so ill a character § as to
whoredom and sodomy that it is not fit to translate it. But those

---

* These words are Bargrave's.     † Vide art. lvii. [J. B.]
‡ Vide art. ix. xv. xxxvi.     § Statera, p. 118.

that understand Italian may read the particulars and their value in that author, where he calleth him *Il gobbo*—*"The crookback," as indeed he was. The picture is very like him, but wanteth his crookt shoulder. J. B.

I, living several summers at Lions in France, had anno 1654 my pention or sojourning in the fair retired place of the Pal Mal of the Bel Court, very near a nunnery, where I grew acquainted with the lady abbess, who had in the nunnery with her two of her nieces, I being often admitted to her particular iron grates and parlour to discourse with her. She was of the noble family of Chatiglion, who were the founders of that nunnery, and by their statutes one of that family was always to be abbess there, if there were any that were capable of it. This lady abbess was very handsome, proper, graceful, well spoken, a *vertuosa*, of excellent parts, much courted by the noblemen, and by this Cardinal Antonio, as she herself told me that he never went between Rome or Paris but he waited upon her. This convent was called La Blée, and she Madame La Blée.

It fortuned, when I was there, that a great disorder fell out in this nunnery, this lady having run herself into ten or twelve thousand pounds of debt, the butchers and bakers and others having trusted her so long that they would trust her no longer, but every one called in for their money, so that the two or three hundred nuns wanted their usual diet, and great factions there were amongst them, and great complaints and appeals were made to their Archbishop, their visitor, who was then a person of great worth and quality, of the noble family (if I be not mistaken) of the Newvills, he being brother, or of very near relation, to the Duke of that name. At the Archbishop's visitation, she pleaded her misfortune came upon her through over-building, she having built a new chapel, a cloister, and a dormitory. The nuns that were against her pleaded that buildings could not have reduced them to such necessities, but that she lavished it away upon two necessitous ranting brothers, and

---

* Statera, p. 116.

others of her kindred and gallants, in luxury and wantonness. In short, she was turned out, and another put into her place, and she was carried as a prisoner, under a guard of soldiers, to another nunnery in the heart of the city, whither I went several times to visit her; where I found her jocund, merry, and cheerful, she still threatening revenge on the Archbishop, saying she knew his ambition, that he aimed at a Cardinal's hat, but that [she] by her friends at the courts of Rome and Paris would hinder him from it, as at length effectually she did.

One day, going to her, I found her wringing her hands, and all in tears; she telling me that, since she had seen me last, she had shed as many tears as that I might bathe in them; that now they sought her life, to cut off her head for false coining of money; and she confessed to me that an Italian had taught her to coin medals, and between them they coined two or three half-crowns, and they had found them in her laboratory. I told her that I was going out of town to Rome, and, if I could serve her there in anything, I would come to receive her commaunds. She thanked me kindly, and told me that she durst not write her mind fully to Cardinal Antonio, because the Archbishop intercepted her letters; but she, having this opportunity, would do it. I accordingly waited upon her, and she committed a packet of letters to me, directed to a confidant of Cardinal Antonio's court; and withal desired me to tell him all particulars how it was with her, and that she had received the 500*l.* that he had sent her since her troubles. I promised her to be faithful in her business, and took my leave of her; and, so soon as I came to Rome, I delivered my letters and message, being very civilly received. Not long after, the Cardinal, under an other pretence of public affairs, went into France, and found the Lady La Blée in prison. He trownced the Archbishop, pleaded the lady's cause in several courts, both civil and ecclesiastic, and at length got the better of it, and restored her to her honour and dignity.

About four years after, I came to Lions again, and waited on her where I first found her; and she was ready to leap through the grates for joy to see me—acknowledging that it was I that help restore her. She had told me that they had accused her of all the sins a woman could commit, and that she was the Cardinal's miss, with all the circumstances (and I believe it); but he overcame it all. J. B. 1662.]

## XIII.

ERNESTUS ADOLBERT TIT. S. PRAESEDIS* S. R. E. PRESB. CARD. AB HARRACH ARCHIEP. PRAGEN. GERMANUS. XIX. JANUAR. MDCXXVI.

La Giusta Statera de' Porporati. [No. xvii. p. 89.]

This Cardinal is by nation a German, or High Dutchman, and rich. He was promoted to the scarlet by Urban the VIII. at the instance of the Emperor. He is a person of great worth and of a good life, being Archbishop of Prague, in Bohemia, to his great praise, and much satisfaction of those people, being much esteemed by his nation for his good qualities and behaviour.

We cannot say much of this subject, because he resideth very little at the Court of Rome, but is always at his Cathedral at Prague. Wherefore with some reason, and not far from the purpose, when Harrach came last to Rome, a little before the death of Urban the VIII., the Pope said this: "Ill news! it is an ill sign for us when we see the *consi* about the city." [What *consi* are I know not, but I suppose them to be some kind of ominous birds or fowl. J. B.†] As if he would say, that Harrach not being accustomed to come to Rome, and he was then come at that time, he foresaw his death to be near; and in effect so it proved.

Harrach careth not much for Italy, finding still there either war or the plague. The Emperor hath a great regard for him, and he, as being his subject, is, and always will be, devoted to the House of

---

* *Sic.*
† Cogan turns the word into "consi," and does not attempt to translate it. Perhaps *corvi*—crows.

Austria. He giveth much alms, is splendid, courteous, and a good housekeeper.

[At the death of Innocent the X<sup>th</sup> I saw him at Rome, when, at the *Sede racante*, he came to the conclave of the election of Alexander the VII., and the year after I saw him again at Prague, where he crowned King of Bohemia the Emperor now reigning. (J. B. 1675.) It is very like him.]

He hath a great aversion to the artifices and dissimulations of the Court of Rome; and once it astonished some of the Cardinals that were present, and had their residence in Rome, to hear with what frankness and integrity he reprehended those iniquities that afflict the Court, and are a scandal to the Church. *Il Cardinalismo, parte* 2, *lib.* 2, *page* 145.

## XIV.

HIERONYMUS TIT. S. MARIAE TRANSTYBORIM S. R. E. CARD<sup>lis</sup> COLUMNA ARCHIPBR' BAS<sup>cae</sup> LATERANEN' ROM. 30 AUGUSTI, 1627.

He is of the\* most noble and most ancient family of Rome, which hath had many Popes and an infinite number of Cardinals. He was promoted by Urban VIII., together with Cardinal Antonio, at the instance of Donna Anna Barberina and the Constable Colonna, by reason of parentage contracted in marriage. He is rich both in the goods of fortune and state. He is wise † and prudent and well esteemed at Court, and reverenced in the Sacred College both for his blood and for his wisdom. He is not displeasing, although he swells and struts it about as if he were another Martin the V.; yet for all that he is courteous and affable and splendid. He loveth the Pope, and the Pope loveth him because he was earnest for him in his election. He was, by Urban VIII<sup>th</sup>, made Archbishop of

Statera de' Porporati. [No. xxxiii. p. 122.]

---

\* Rather " of *a* most noble," &c. (*di*, not *della*). † "Savio."

Bologna, which dignity, when he had kept it a while, he resigned it in the time of Innocent the X[th].

Although there be matches of marriage between the two families of Colonna and Barbarini, yet there is no great friendship between them for private interesses. Don Carlo Colonna, brother to the Cardinal, treacherously killed Don Gregorio Gaetano, brother to the Duke of Sermoneta,* for which he was condemned to death by Urban the VIII. But, for the Cardinal's sake, he was not only reprieved, but also, to defend him from the revenge of the Gaetanos' malice, he was first made a Benedictine monk, and afterwards an Archbishop *in partibus infidelium* [a fine Roman trick, to protect a murtherer!—to make him a titular Bishop or Archbishop in a kingdom where he hath nothing to do, having no authority there; and this shall be his security in Italy.

He is of the Spanish faction. The picture is very like him. J. B. 1672.]

## XV.

JOANN. BAPTISTA TIT. S. PETRI AD VINCULA S. R. E. PR'BR. CARD. PALLOTTUS PICENUS. XIX NOVEMB. MDCXXIX.

La Statera de' Porporati. [No. xxv. p. 131.]

He is of a worthy family of Calderola, in the Marca of Ancona, and nephew to the late Cardinal Palotto; who is, as his uncle was, a great enemy to thieves. He is very well as to goods of fortune—his uncle leaving him good inheritances.

He put himself into the prelature, and was employed in several charges by Urban the VIII., and, in particular, he was by him made Governor of Rome, in which office he carried himself with great decorum, and satisfaction to the people, being just and severe, to

---

* The enmity between these great families dates from the pontificate of Boniface VIII. (Benedict Gaetani), A.D. 1294.

the displeasure of the Pope's nephews;* as for instance:—In the time of Carnival [a month or so before Lent, when all Italy seem to be mad, J. B.†] a proclamation is usually made for several orders of that time; whereof one was, that no woman should wear any mask or be in mascarade in the Curso, under pain of being sent to prison, and to be there whipt, and other punishment reserved to the Governor. Notwithstanding this order, the famous courtesan (or whore) Checa Buffona was often seen mascaraded in the Curso, and was warned to be gone and come no more; but she would not obey. Upon which Palotto, being angry, presently sent her to prison, and ordered her to be publicly whipt about the city, and, to hinder all recommendations for her by friends, he retired, and gave order that nobody should come to him in two hours, for which time he locked himself up in his study; in which time a gentleman came to him from Cardinal Antonio, the Pope's domineering nephew (whose courtizan among the rest she was‡). This gentleman made a great deal of stir and noise until the two hours were past, and then he did his message—which was, an order from Cardinal Antonio to him to set Checa Buffona at liberty. To which Palotto answered, his eminence was *Patron*, and it should be done so soon as justice was done. But, when the Governor's order for her release came to the prison, Checa had already been whipt, which Antonio hearing, for madness he stamped his foot upon the ground, and grievously threatened revenge; which danger Palotto foreseeing, went and told all the business to his uncle the Pope, who commended him for what he had done. But yet he, knowing Antonio's revengeful spirit, would take away the occasion, and prevent the inconvenience that might follow; and therefore removed Palotto, and sent him his Collector-general into the kingdom of Portogall; where he, staying

* "Faceva poco conto delli neputi di sua Beatitudine."
† A learned German Jesuit professor in the Collegio Romano said to the editor in the beginning of Lent, " Die Narreszeit ist vorüber!"
‡ Vide art. xii. [J. B.] [See the Stat or, p. 118.]

some months, took upon him, to maintain some ecclesiastical jurisdiction, to excommunicate all the King's Council at Lisbon, which was the cause that he was fain to make his escape out of a window, and, to salve himself, to fly privately to Rome.

At his return he was for several respects promoted to a Cardinal's cap. The first was, to put him out of the danger of Antonio's revenge; the second was, for his merits—his Holiness knowing him to be a man of great parts and knowledge. But Antonio was still a thorn in his side, doing him all the displeasures he could, especially in the difference he had with the General of the Augustines, whom Palotto thought to chastise and mortify for many faults that he had committed. But Antonio protected and defended him, and, in spite of Palotto, procured an apostolic order to confirm him in the generalship vii. years longer.

He is very papable, and esteemed worthy by all, especially the princes that know his virtue and qualities, being a man of an angelical life; and Rome would be glad to see him Pope, to pull down the pride of the Barberini. Innocent the X$^{th}$ now reigning hath a great regard for him, though his kindred care not for him, because he speaketh his mind freely of them to the Pope. One day the Pope asked him what the city of Rome thought or said of him? To whom Palotto answered, "Most Holy Father, the city and everybody murmur extraordinarily to see you led away so by your sister-in-law Donna Olimpia, and she should be, as it were, perpetually at court." To whom the Pope answered, "We will remedy it." Donna Olympia coming a while after to court, the Pope told her what Palotto had said to him, and therefore he desired her to abstain from coming so often to the Apostolic pallace. Upon this, Donna Olympia took such a hatred against Palotto, that upon all occasions she affronted him to his face;* which Palotto seeing, he asked leave to retire into his own country, and it was given out at

* "Che un giorno incontrandosi insieme elli, gli chiuse in faccia la bandinella della carozza."

the court that he was sent to visit the fortifications of Marriana and the Marca Ancona.*

He is very affable and obliging, doing courtesies, when it is in his power, very heartily. He hath several nephews, but he is his beloved that is a student in the English College, and would certainly be the Cardinal Patrone if his uncle should come to be Pope. This Cardinal seemeth to be newter as to France or Spain; but it is thought that he is immovably for the house of Austria.

[When I went first of my four times to Rome, there were there four revolters to the Roman Church that had been fellows of Peter-house in Cambridge with myself. The name of one of them was Mr. R. Crashaw, who was of the *Seguita* (as their term is; that is, an attendant, or one of the followers,) of this Cardinal; for which he had a salary of crowns by the month (as the custom is), but no diet. Mr. Crashaw infinitely commended his Cardinal, but complained extremely of the wickedness of those of his retinue; of which he, having the Cardinal's ear, complained to him. Upon which the Italians fell so far out with him that the Cardinal, to secure his life, was fain to put him from his service, and procuring him some small imploy at the Lady's of Loretto; whither he went in pilgrimage in summer time, and, overheating himself, died in four weeks after he came thither, and it was doubtful whether he were not poisoned.†

I have seen Palotto very devout, almost to tears, when he hath been a-washing and wiping some pilgrims' feet. (J. B. 1662.) The picture is very like him.]

---

* " Di Marina nella Marca."
† The death of Crashaw (well known as a poet) took place in 1650. (Chalmers's Biogr. Dictionary.)

## XVI.

FRAN<sup>us</sup> MAR<sup>a</sup> BRANCACCIUS TIT. SS. XII. APOST. S. R. E.
PRES' CARD. EPIS. VITERB. NEAP<sup>us</sup>. 28 NOVEMB. 1633.

*La Statera [No. xxxi. p. 149.]*

He is a Neapolitan gentleman. He was bishop of the city of Capuccio in that kingdom, where, upon some cause about ecclesiastical jurisdiction, he was at discord with a captain of Spanish Foot, sent thither by the Vice-king of Naples. From words they came to arms, and the captain was killed by the bishop's (*castrato*) eunuch;[*] upon which the Vice-king cited him to appear before him, to give him an accoumpt of this homicide. Brancaccio obeyed, and went to Naples; but the same night, to avoid the appearance at a laic king's court, bethought himself, fled in a felucca [a boat about as big as a Gravesend barge, J. B.] towards Rome, and, being arrived, he told the whole business to Urban the VIII.; who, by the inward hatred he had to the Spaniards, did not only commend him, but undertook to defend him. Which the Vice-king seeing, he sequestered all the revenues of his bishoprick; and this poor prelate lived in a great deal of penury and want at Rome.

When his process in law was ended, and he was absolved by the Pope, he had[†] leave to return to his church, but the Vice-king opposed him, charging them with rebellion that did receive him and assist him, saying that his Majesty of Spain did expect that his Holiness should put another into his place. At that time the Pope had daily thoughts to fill up the vacant cardinals' places. The Colonni at one side, the Barbarini on the other, were for this man, and that man, and t'other man; but the Pope took the proverb, *Inter duos litigantes tertius gaudet*, and therefore he, without any of their recommendations, pitched upon Brancaccio in despite of the Spaniards, to whom he was much contrary.

[*] The original says that the bishop "gli fece tirare un' archibugiata dal suo castratto."
[†] "Prese."

He, being now a prince of the Holy Church, was as so to be reverenced and honoured, and the Pope restored him to his bishopric; upon which he went to Naples, where he met with two other cardinals—Aldobrandino, for his pleasure, to see some great pastimes for the joy of the birth of a prince in Spain, and Boncompagni, Archbishop of the place. There Brancaccio stayed some months, until the Count of Monte-Real, the then Vice-king, commanded him presently to be gone,* not only out of the city, but out of the kingdom. So the poor Cardinal was forced to return with his whole family to Rome, where the Pope gave him the bishopric of Viterbo, and procured him many pentions.

Innocent the $X^{th}$ careth not much for him, because of a contest between him and Donna Olympia, the Pope's sister-in-law, who is of Viterbo;† and in a word, to conclude, he is poor and proud. [The picture is like him. J. B. 1677.]

## XVII.

VLDERICUS TIT. S. ANASTASIAE S. R. E. PR'BR. CARD. CARPINEUS URBINATEN. XXVIII. NOVEMB. MDCXXXIII.

This Cardinal is a nobleman of the city of Urbino. He was a poor prelate, but Francesco Barbarino, imploying him in some affairs, liked him well, and took an affection to him, and upon his request he was made Cardinal, for which he is likewise grateful to that family. The Lord Conte of Carpegna, his brother, is constantly imployed in the wars against the princes of Italy.‡ He is a man of weak parts, but laborious and toilsome, and amongst others may pretend to scarlet.§ Although the Cardinal pretend neutrality, [La Statera de' Porporati. [No. xxx. p. 148].

---

* "Gli presentò una carta di sua Maestà Cattolica, nella quale ordinava," &c.
† "Poiche lui inconsideratamente si è dimostrato troppo interessato in alcuni differenze di territorii, tra quelli della sua chiesa e quelli di Donna Olimpia, che sono nella città di Viterbo."
‡ "assistè continuamente nella guerra d' Urbano contro li prencipi d' Italia."
§ "potrebbe un giorno haver speranza nelle comuni pretensioni de porporati."

yet his affection is more for the French. He is a studious, melancholy man, and free to his power to his brothers, whereof one is the Conte, and the other Canon of S<sup>ta</sup> Maria Inviolata.\*

[I was told that this Conte Carpegna married an English lady, of the family of the Dudleys, who pretend to the dukedom of Northumberland, earldom of Warwick, &c., and are acknowledged as such by the Pope and Emperor. I met with her father at Florence, who was much esteemed by the Grand Duke; whilst I was there he put forth a very ingenious book, in a thin folio, "Dell Arcano dell Mare."† Afterward I met with his eldest son, a traveller, at Orleans in France; and in a convent at Angeers, in the chapel, I read upon a wall all the English titles of honour over the grave of his younger son, who was basely murthered there in his travels. J. B. 1677.

This picture is not very like him.] The family of the Medici, the Great Duke of Tuscany, are much his friends, and he a most partial one to them. But, those Cardinals being since dead, he had none to promote him in the last conclave.

> Carpegna c' ha [una] debil complessione
> Si tien spedito, perche questa volta
> Li Medici non fanno ordinatione.‡

"Carpegna's of a weak complexion,
And may despair of his election,
Since Medici give no direction."

Il Cardinalismo, page 149 [148].

---

\* Sic MS. (for "In via Lata.")

† For the remarkable history of this Sir Robert Dudley, son (whether legitimate or not is doubtful) of the Earl of Leicester, see Dugdale, Baronage, ii. 225; Wood, Athenæ Oxon. ed. Bliss, iii. 258; Biogr. Britannica, iii. 1807; Craik, Romance of the Peerage, iii. 87, sqq. The emperor did not affect to overrule the English decision against his claim to the dukedom of Northumberland, but himself created him a duke.

‡ "Terzetti," p. 290. See above, p. 16. It will be seen that the point of the verses is missed in the translation.

## XVIII.

ASCANIUS TIT. S. MARIAE DE ARACOELI S. R. E. PR'PR'.* CARD. PHILAMARIN. NEAPOLITAN. ARCHIEP. NEAP. XVI. DECEMB. MDCXLI.

He was by Urban VIII. made Cardinal, and Arch[bishop of] Naples. Though the service he had done the Church did scarce deserve a simple canonicate, yet Urban promoted him because he had done most eminent service to the Barbarines, his family; and, indeed, in this Urban cannot but be thanked for enriching the Church with a person adorned with so many excellent qualities, which made him worthy of the Popedom itself, having since this his elevation edified not only his flock but all Christendom besides, and rendered most singular service to the House of Austria in the revolt of Naples and the business of Massaniello, 1647. [Of this last passage at Naples, I that wrote this was an eye witness. J. B. 1672.] Il Nipotismo, p. 92, pt. i. l. 3.

He is a Neapolitan gentleman, of a small place called Chianchi-sella, subject to Benivento. He was very poor, and, to remedy his miseries, he came to the Court of Rome, and presented himself to a Cardinal that was his countryman, to help him to some imploy; who got him to be chief chamberlain to Cardinal Maffeo Barbarino, whose two geniuses met so well together in the delight of astrology that the Cardinal had a great love for him. Gregory the XV<sup>th</sup> dying, that Cardinal Maffeo, in the next conclave, was chosen Pope, in the name of Urban the VIII., who, so soon as he had made his nephew, Francesco Barbarino, Cardinal, he placed Filomarini with him as superintendent, and to help him and wait on him as his *maestro di camera*, with authority to wear a purple gown;† for the Cardinal was but young, and as yet fitter to be governed than to govern. But after a while the Cardinal growing up could not La Giusta Statera de' Porporati. [No. xl. p. 188.]

---

* *Sic.*  † "con autorità di puoter vestir di pavonazzo."

indure to see himself tutored by his chamberlain, [and] would have put him out of his retinue but that he was protected by the Pope, his uncle, who promised him to promote him. But the Cardinal, that hated him, still kept him from promotion, under pretence that he could not be without him, whereas the truth was that he scorned or hated to see him made his equal.

It happened that the archbishoprick of Naples fell void by the death of Cardinal Buoncompagno. Philamarini put in for it after twenty-four years'* service in the family; to whom the Pope answered that that place was fitter for a Cardinal than for him; which saying put him into a fever, and still the nephew hindered him, until at length a day of promotion was held, and doubtful it was who should have the cap. But it fell upon this Philomarin, who was saluted by the term of "Your Eminence," and had withal the archbishoprick of Naples.

He is very high-minded and proud. [The picture is very like him. J. B.]

## XIX.

F. Vincentius Maculanus Ord. Praedicatorum tit. S. Clemen. Card. S. Clementis Nuncupatus de Florentiola Placen. Dioces. xiii. Xbris, mdcxli.

*Out of an Italian Manuscrip.†*   A native of Fiorenzola, in the state of Piacenza, of a rustic ignoble family. He was a brother of the Dominican order. He was first made by Urban VIII. Commissary of the Holy Office, in which he was a severe man. Then he was made Master of the Sacred Pallace. The war breaking out between the Barbarini (that is, the Pope with his nephews) and the Princes of Italy, this man

---

\* The original has "28."

† "Supplimenti d'alcuni Cardinali che sono ommessi nella Statera in stampa." (See the Introduction to this volume.) fol. 19 *sqq.*

was very active and diligent, especially in the business of fortifications, so that he ruined many fine places and villas, delitious pallaces, both ancient and modern, to make way for his fortifications; whereby he got the good will of the Pope, but a deadly hatred of the nobility and people.

He hath several brothers, who, being rude clowns, never come to Court;* but he breedeth up two of his little nephews with affection and kindness, teaching them how they may grow rich by their industry.† When he was brother of the order, he was much beholden to Mons$^r$ Foppa, of Bergamo, to whom his Eminence afterward, in recompence, resigned his archbishoprick of Benevento, in the kingdom of Naples, but a feouditary to the Church.

He is hated to death, as I said before, because of his many fortifications, by which the Pope imposeth many taxes and other grievances, with which they will ruin the ecclesiastic state with new impositions. The Matthei could drink his blood for his taking away half the famous villa of that family for his useless fortifications and architecture. It may be said of this Maculano, that he bought his red hat with the price of human blood, being cruel when he was Commissary, in the death of the priest Barbane, who had been confessor to Pope Gregory the XV. He made also die in prison the Abbot of St. Praxede, who, living there many years, yet was not permitted the least change of linen; and all for no other fault proved against him but his being a faithful friend to the Great Duke of Toscany.

He is an arrogant man, and pretends to the papacy; and, that he may be thought to be an almsgiver, he doth it on certain days [of] the week, too publicly and vaingloriously.‡ [The picture is like

---

\* " non ha voluto che si facessero veder alla Corte."

† " e per accommodarli in qualche ricchezza, usaria etiandio industria rusticale e venale."

‡ " pocho elemosinario, mà perche pretende al Papato, si dimostra hoggi amico delli poveri, facendovi alcuni giorni della settimana far circolo delli poverelli nella sua casa, accio sia tenuto per elemosinario."

him, he always going in black, in his Dominican habit, never putting on his purple or his scarlet. J. B. 1662.

I have several times been at Fiorenzola, between Bolonia and Florence.]

## XX.

JULIUS TIT. S. PRISCAE S. R. E. PR'BR. CARD. GABRIELLUS EP'US ASCULANUS, ROMAN. XVI DECEMB. MDCXLI.

La Giusta Statura de' Porporati. [No. xxxix. p. 186].

He is a noble Roman, was Clerk of the Apostolic Chamber, and was promoted by Urban the VIII. that the place might be sold to another. He is now a poor Cardinal, being (as it were) banished to a miserable bishoprick loaden with pensions, in the city of Ascoli, in the Marca Ancona. The best part of his convenience he acknowledgeth to receive from the family of the Lancelloti. He hath received many disgusts from the Barbarini, but knoweth not how to ease himself. He fayneth to be devoted to the house of Austria, but is inwardly for the French. He is an intelligent, studious, curious man; affable in treatises;* but he is poor, and cannot give much alms. He is of a retired good life, hath no enemies in the Sacred College, and at the Court his presence is accepted. He hath some nephews of no ill parts, and is related to many noble families, and in particular to the Lancelloti, the Altieri, and the Coccini, all Romans. This Cardinal in his bishoprick hath had many differences, so that they have been ready tumultuously to revolt against him about imposition of taxes.

Il Cardinalismo, p. 114.

He was promoted to the Cardinal dignity without any merits of his own, only that his clerkship of the Chamber might be sold. In the time that he was legate of Urban, he shewed no small rapacity or (to give it a milder term) avidity. So it is that by his parsimony and other ways he hath known how to inrich his own family vastly,

"affabile nel trattar che fa."

and would do it more should he come to be Pope; but there is no great probability of that now. The people of his diocese are not well satisfied with him—not for any defect in the exercise of his pastoral cure, but because he pressed and exacted several taxes that were imposed by the Pope. His virtues are, that, being conscious [*] of his own ignorance, he indeavoureth what he can to improve himself by conversing with learned men, in whose company he is very affable, but something too ceremonious. Some there are that look upon him as malicious and revengeful; and truly I think him so in weighty matters, but not in small things, which he passeth over.

[The picture is like him. J. B. 1674.]

## XXI.

COESAR[†] TIT. SS. QVATVOR CORONOTOR.[†] S. R. E. PR'BR CARD. FACHENETTUS, EP'US SPOLET. BONONIEN. XIII JVLII, MDCXLIII.

He is a nobleman of Bologna, nephew to Innocent the IX. He was a worthy prelate, and therefore sent nuntio to the Catholick King; at the end of which charge he was promoted to the purple by Urban the VIII., and then first made bishop of Senegalla, an ancient city and port in the state of Urbino, where he was observed to be a good and vigilant man, being very charitable, and beloved of his flock. He hath no enemies in the Sacred College, but is beloved of them all. He is not very old, but hereafter he may arrive at St. Peter's Chair, and the rather, because he is devoted to the house of Austria. He hath no considerable vices; the Pope's family have a regard for him. If he should be propounded by the head of a faction, the Spaniards would be for his election; he would be no ill Pope for the good of the Church.

Innocent the X[th] hath given his brother the charge of the militia in the Romagna, and that man would reign if his brother should be

La Statera de' Porporati. [No. xliv. p. 209.]

---

[*] MS. Bargrave, "confident."      [†] Sic.

Pope, for he hath no considerable blemishes but one, that he is too much in love with a Roman lady called Nina Barcarola. The family is wholly for the Spaniards.

He hath no Cardinals his enemies in the whole College. The Spaniards are his friends, and the French have no reason to complain on him; his merits also are so great, that if the See were vacant, he would have no small party for his election. But the mischief is, an unlucky custom that is lately introduced, and that is, that the nephews of the last Pope will have one of their own creatures to succeed him. *Il Cardinalismo*, p. 151. [The picture is something, but not very, like him. J. B. 1662.]

## XXII.

HIERONYMUS TIT. S. TRINITAT. IN MONTE PINCIO S. R. E. PRESB. CARD. GRIMALDUS ARCHIEP. AGVEN. GENVEN. XIII. IVLII. MDCXLIII.

La Statera de' Porporati. [No. xliii. p. 204.]

He is a nobleman of Genoüa, and near of kin to the prince of Monte Honorato. He was a souldier, serving the Emperor in Germany, and at his return he put on the long robe, and bought the place of one of the masters of the Chamber.* He was by Urban the VIII. made Governor of Rome, in which charge he carried himself well, to the great satisfaction of the people.

At the end of that government he was sent nuntio into France, and at his return he was promoted to the purple, for two respects; the one was, to get money for his chamberlain's place; the other was, to promote a French nuncio. Some say it was he that negotiated the revolt from the Spaniards by his kinsman the Prince of Monaco; but others say that it was one Monsù di Bordon, a Frenchman of the family of Grimaldi, there being many of that family in France; but it cannot be denied but that the Cardinal had a great

---

* "il chiericato della Camera."

stroke in the business. The cause of that revolution was, that the Prince of Monaco had, upon conditions with the King of Spain, took him for his protector, and received into the place a Spanish garrison, and so it continued for some years. But at lenght, the ministers of Spain neglecting to pay the garrison, and the agreement with the Prince, the Prince, being poor, and not able to maintain the garrison, was forced privately to treat with the King of France, to bring in a French garrison there, and to surprise the Spaniards unawares, and send the starved poor flock of them home to their master of the Golden Fleece,* which was compassed (with no small difficulty) by this Cardinal's subtle and prudential carriage; for which Urban the VIII. promoted him to the cap, and for other services done to the apostolic seat.

He is well as to the goods of fortune, but too low as to his quality and splendid mind.† He is very affable and courteous to all persons, according to their condition.‡ He and his family are under the protection of France. He is knowing and studious. The King of France made him comprotector of that nation in the absence of Cardinal Antonio, in which imploy he got the Pope's displeasure, having too openly spoken in favour of the Barbarini; for which the Pope oftentimes refused him audience. As he is of a princely family he is esteemed at Court, and as a nobleman of Genoüa, and is beloved of most.

[The picture is like him. J. B.]

---

* "fù sforzato di scacciar il presidio Spagniolo, e introdur il Francese, havendo giudicato esserli di maggiore utile, restituendo al Cattolico la smagrita pecorella del toson d'oro."

† "E comodo di beni di fortuna, mà non ricco, per che secondo il suo stato è povero; è splendido d'animo."

‡ "Honora tutti senza eccettione di persona alcuna."

## XXIII.

### ANGELUS TIT. SS. QUIRICI ET JULITE S. R. E. PRESB. CARD. GIORIUS. CAMERS. XIII. JVLY, MDCXXXXIII.

*La Statera de'*
*Porporati.*
*[No. li. p. 229.]*

He is a native of the city Camerino, of vile progeny; but he kept a small school in Rome,* which he left to serve Cardinal Maffeo Barberino, to wait upon his nephews as a pedant (that is, Francesco, Antonio, and Tadeo), conducting them every day to school to the Roman College and bringing them back again. And, being imployed in many other things in that family, he carried himself with so much diligence that he gained the love of his patron. It so fell out Maffeo was chosen Pope, and Giorio was made a prelate, in which place he thrived so well that in a short time he got a good revenue. And Urban the VIII., his patron, to reward him for his several good offices he had done,† promoted him to the purple.

He hath brothers and nephews, which are never seen at Court by reason of their base condition and clownishness. He is much delighted in hunting, which all the Barbarinos, especially the Pope, loved. This Cardinal, being raised by the Barbarini from nothing, must be always of the French side against the House of Austria. He is of a robust age, and not very old. The Sacred College hath no great esteem of him; but in the Court he is looked upon as a rich Cardinal, and one that will do anything to get money. His parts are but mean, being chiefly exercised in nothing but pedantry.‡ [The picture is like him. J. B. 1664.]

---

\* " In Roma povero prete, lasciando la publica scuola che lui esercitava."

† " E essendo stato per lungo tempo assiduamente alli servitii Urbani, parce a sua beatitudine non fargli torto," &c.

‡ " Nella corte vien stimato come porporato e pecuniario in modo che per accumular danari essercitarebbe ogni venalità. Altro non ha di buono questi soggetto, ch' è meno ignorante degli altri servidori d' Urbano, per essersi esercitato del continuo nella pedanteria." The French ambassador is more favourable, " Buon uomo e buon cacciatore, . . . . e lodevole per la sua schiettezza." Fol. 42-3.

## XXIV.

JOANNES E SOCIETATE JESU TIT. S. BALBINAE S. R. E. PRESB. CARD. DE LUGO HISPALEN. XIII. JVLII, MDCXLIII.

He is a Spanish gentleman. He was a Jesuit, and a perfect theologian. He, satisfying Urban the VIII. in divers occurrences, was made a Cardinal by him for his reward. He is a man of a good, exemplary life; but I am vexed that he was a Jesuit, and a schoolmaster of the College; *et hoc sufficit*. Some say that he was assisted by those of his society; others say no, for he seemeth to show himself no great friend to the Jesuits. His parents and relations supplied him; besides he had heaped up some money by the Jesuits' way—*cum cantionibus et aliis adminiculis*—with taking of pawnes, &c.

[La Giusta Statera de' Porporati. No. lvii. p. 240.]

Of his family have been many learned men.[*] By reason of the obligation he hath to the Barberini, in the conclave he seemed to be of their faction for France; but in conclusion, by a stratagem he had, he gave his voice for the Spaniard; and after the election of Innocent the X[th], he separated himself wholly from the Barberini, and verified the common saying, *Esser ingrato come Giesuita*—"To be as ungrateful as a Jesuit."[†]

[I being at Rome in the *sede vacante* at Innocent the X[th]'s death. 1655, in the conclave several days we heard sometimes this Cardinal, sometimes that, was to be Pope; and for a day or two the vogue ran that Cardinal Lugo was like to be the man. Upon which wagers were proffered *pro* and *con.*, some being for him, some against him. The arguments against him were twofold, affirmative and negative—affirmative, because that he was a Jesuit, and they

---

[*] "La sua nascita è civile, e ha havuto nella sua casa molti huomini in lettere insigni."

[†] The French ambassador says, "Lugo è Giesuita e Spagnuolo, due raggioni per le quali V. E. non può fidarsene. E' gran Theologo, e che prattica la sua scienza, vivendo esemplarmente, à consolattione de' letterati e edificazione della Corte." Fol. 13.

were sure the conclave would never choose a Jesuit, lest St. Peter's infallible chair should never be recovered out of their hands; and therefore the Popes are careful not to make Jesuits Cardinals, lest their votes should be too many at an election of a Pope in the conclave. The negative argument against him was, because he was not an Italian; because that Clement the V$^{th}$, a French Cardinal, being chosen Pope, he carried St. Peter's chair into France to Avignon, where it continued about 70 years in the hands of six or seven successive Popes that were all Frenchmen, until at lenght, the Italians being weary of making their appeals and long journeys into France, Pope Gregory the XI$^{th}$ was forced to translate the chair, and carry it again to Rome. Upon this, the Italians have ever since taken care that St. Peter's chair shall never be a tramontan chair again; and therefore now none but Italians are papable.

It is like him if the beard were not so long. J. B. 1677.]

## XXV.

VIRGINIUS S. MARIAE IN VIALATA S. R. E. DIACONVS CARD. VRSINVS ROMANVS. XVI. X$^{BRIS}$ MDCXXXXI.

La Statera de' Porporati. [No. xxxviii. p. 181.]

He is of noble birth, being nephew to the Duke of Bracciano, and brother to the Duke of Santo Gemini. He was but an abbot, and thought to leave his clerical habit, and to marry the Princess Lodovisia. But Pope Urban, not liking that conjunction of blood, broke off the match by making him a Cardinal. Others say, his uncle the Duke lost at play,* and gave to Cardinal Antonio, the Pope's nephew, great sums of gowld to make his nephew a Cardinal. But the truth is, his merits and the antiquity of his family deserved a Cardinal's cap, which can count as many purples as there are days;† the house of the Ursini having with arms defended the Apos-

---

\* There is no mention of losses at play in the original.

† " che racconta più porpore che giorni."

tolic seat in its greatest dangers.* Only a Cardinal of this family and of that of Colonna † have place in the chapel with imbassadors; but, because of a dispute about precedency, they never both appear at a time, there having been war and great differences between these two families.

Innocent the X$^{th}$ had a very great familiarity and kindness for him and his uncle the Duke; but now they are fallen out about the principality of Piumbino, and the Cardinal hath put up the French King's arms over his pallace, as taking him for his protector. He is looked upon as a splendid but very proud man, ready to give affronts, but to receive none.‡ He is a man of great resentment and revenge, being feared at court, and reverenced by the college.

This Cardinal hath had above 300 Cardinals in his family.§ It is more an honour to the college to have him a Cardinal, than it is an honour to him to be a Cardinal. Some people believe him vindicative; but his anger is only a soden impetus, not lasting or durable at all. And he is unjustly aspersed with pride; for he is very civil to all persons that come near him, and particularly obliging in his letters, which he vouchsafeth to return in very familiar language to all that write to him, especially [if] they be of any quality.

Il Cardinalismo, p. [149.] 150.

## XXVI.

JULIUS S .... S. R. E. PRIMUS DIACONUS CARDINALIS MAZA-
RINUS ROMANUS.  XVI DECEMB. MDCXLI.

La Giusta Statera de' Porporati. [No. xxxiv. p. 166.]

He is the son of Peter Mazzarini, a Sicilian, a broken merchant,

---

\* " Havendo loro antenati pugnato e tenuto lontani li Barbari da Roma, mantenendo la sede apostolica con molta sicurezza."

† " Questa casata com' anco quella di Colonna,"—nothing being said of Cardinals.

‡ " E per causa di precedenza fece affronto con farli fermar la carozza, e maltrattar la famiglia del residente della defonta regina di Francia, Maria de' Medici."

§ The number of Orsini Cardinals in Chacon's Index is 27, so that the estimate in the text must be understood as extending to connexions of other names.

that failed for a considerable sum of money, and therefore fled from thence to Rome with all his family, where this Giulio and his brother were born. The latter was made a Dominican, and as they changed places so they changed fortunes. Giulio waited some time upon the nephews of the Cardinal Colonna, after that he was of the *Seguita* (as the term is) or retinue of Cardinal Sacchetti,* in his money affairs, with which he trafficked, and got no small sum for himself in gaming. Then for a while he was a souldier, but, returning to the court, he was again of Sacchetti's followers; whose great kindness to him made him prefer him to Cardinal Antonio, who made him a prelate by the Pope his uncle's favour; by whom he was sent Apostolic nuntio into Savoy, and to take *in deposito* for the Pope the strong city of Casale, in the marquisate of Montferrat, out of the hands of the French. So that, according to an agreement, the Spaniards and the High Dutch should quit Mantoüa, of which they had possession, because that Duke had declared himself for the French, and denied to be feudatory to the Emperor; for which he was made Duke of Nivers in France.†

Mazzarino went, and causing the French, according to agreement, to march out, he took the city of Casale *in deposito* for his Holiness. Upon which the Spaniards and Highgermans quitted Mantoüa, and delivered it up to that Duke; which was no sooner done but Mazzarino let the French in again into Cassal; whereby the Pope, the Emperor, and the Spaniard were fooled and baffled, and new bloody wars grew upon it in Montferrat, Milan, Savoy, and Piedmont.

This treacherous dealing of Mazzarino brought him in great favour with the Cardinal of Richlieu and the King of France, they thinking him a fit man for the designs of that crown; whereupon he was received into that court and counsell, the Most Christian King writing to the Pope to make him a Cardinal for the good service he had done. But the Pope denied it, saying that he had wronged him, as

---

\* Vide art. x. [J. B.]
† " perch' era stato dal Rè di Francia dechiarato Duca de Nivers."

well as the Emperor and King of Spain, in that business of Casall; but withal told the King of France that, if he pleased to nominate some other subject for to be Cardinal, he would grant it. But the Most Christian King obstinately persisted in his demand for Mazzarino, which Urban seeing, he could do no less than to content his Majesty in it; and so he was made a Cardinal.

After the death of Cardinal Richlieu, the chief minister of the crown of France, this Cardinal succeeded in his command; but the goodwill and bounty of his patron made him to be hated of all the great ones in France, pretenders to that great place. However, the King honoured him exceedingly, making him one of the Parliament and Counsellor of State, and, at his death, left him to be one of the executors of his last will and testament.

He is grown so rich that no feudatory prince is wealthier than he. He often desired of his Majesty in his lifetime that he might return to Rome, and take his Cardinal's hat of Urban the VIII.;* but the King would never give him leave. He grew so great that all the princes of the blood were fain to be commanded by him; upon which they plotted against his life, to take him off by a violent death; but he still discovered all their secret designs, so that many of them, for his sake, were put to death, others fled and were banished, others imprisoned, until at lenght it brake out into a civil war against the government, and the princes would not lay down their arms until Mazzarino was banished the court and kingdom, which the Queen Regent would not yield unto. But Mazzarino raised forces against the princes, and so the war went on until an agreement was made between the princes and him.

He was very busy against the election of Pope Innocent the X[th], which when he could not hinder, he sent great forces into Italy, and affrighted the Pope [taking the Barbarini into the French King's

---

* "Domandato più volte licenza à quelle maestà di poter tornar in Roma, e prender capello à tempo ch' era vivo Urbano."

protection].* Upon which the Catholic King declared him and all his relations rebels and traitors, as being Sicilians.†

While he was a souldier he was a vicious gamester, and upon a woman's accoumpt had received many wounds; but since he grew great he grew very grave, and very grateful to those who had formerly obliged him, especially to the defence of the Barbarini. He made his young brother General of the Dominican order,‡ Master of the Sacred Palace, Archbishop of Aix in France, and, at last, Cardinal; in all which dignities he died a young man. [J. B. 1677.

I have often seen his old father at Rome, who, by his son's favour (as there I heard), was, for his accoumpt and honour, made a nobleman of Venice, who are treated with the title of "Your Excellency." He used to go about the streets of Rome with but a coach and two horses, with six *staffiery* or servants in livery to walk by his coach side, as the mode is there.

Il Conte Gualdo Priorato§ hath written in Italian ten books of the Revolutions of France, where all the intrigues of Mazzarino are mentioned. I made an acquaintance with that author at the shop in Venice where his book in folio, "Appresso Paolo Baglioni," is sold, MDCLV. He held great correspondence, first with the Parliament, then with Oliver Cromwell, then with his son Richard,

---

* Vide art. xii. [J. B.]

† The French ambassador writes, "Già sà 'l mondo che Mazzarino è 'l miraculo de' nostri tempi, l' eroe di questo seculo, la gloria dell' Italia, e la reputattione della Francia. Non ha bisogno de' miei elogij, e V. E. può meglio ammirar la sua virtù di quello ch' io sappia e possa descrivere." Fol. 50-1.

‡ "Con la sua auttorità fece che di giovenile età il suo fratello forse eletto Generale della religione Domenicana."

§ Vide art. xxxix. [J. B.] [Galeazzo Gualdo Priorato, Count of Comazzo, was born at Vicenza in 1606, and died there in 1678. Although largely engaged in active life, he was a very voluminous author. "On comprend difficilement comment Gualdo Priorato a pu trouver le temps d'écrire autant d'ouvrages qu'il en a publiés." Biog. Générale, ed. Hoefer.]

against the King, as you may see in Milton's Latin letters to him in their names. Then he caused King Charles the II^d and the rest of the royal family to be banished France. And another Italian author,* that writeth a history of our late civil wars of England, saith that King Charles the First suspected Mazzarino and the imbassador of France had a hand in his troubles, " for reasons that I could tell (saith that author), but it is not fit for me to speak them."† So that we may almost more than probably conclude that our war was a religious war, fomented from Rome.‡ Mazzarino in France, Rossetti the Pope's nuntio in England, and Gio-Bat. Rinuccini the Archbishop of Firmo in Italy, but nuntio in Ireland, were the ecclesiastics, and the embassadors of France and Spain the Romanist seculars, that worked the war and confusion amongst us—so that the King and Archbishop Lawd died martyrs for their Protestant religion.

I have seen pictures more like him. J. B.]

## XXVII.

RAYNALDVS S. NICOLAI IN CARCERE TVLLIANO S. R. E. DIACON' CARD. ESTENS. EP'VS REGIENS. MVTINENS. XVI. DECEMB. MDCXLI.

This Cardinal is a prince, as being brother to the Duke of Modena. He was promoted to the purple at the request of the Emperor to Urban the VIII., after which the war of Italy happened between the princes of Italy and the Barberini, the Pope and his nephews, chiefly against the Duke of Parma. Upon this occasion this prince would never go to Rome to have his Cardinal's hat put on by Urban whilst his nephews reigned; which afterwards he received from Innocent the X^th, being at the conclave at his election. [La Statera de' Porporati. (No. xxxii. p. 155.)]

---

* Il Conte Bisaccione, edit. 2ª, p. 55. [J. B.] (ed. 4, p. 53; see above, p. 17.)
† This seems a very free translation of " per raggioni che qui non è luogo di introdurre."
‡ Vide art. viii. [J. B.]

After his being some months at Rome, it happened * that the Austrian faction had many meetings about business of that crown at the pallace of Albornoz, to which his Eminence was never called or invited, as if they did not confide in him. One day there was a consistory to be held about the interesses of Portugal, as to the providing for those churches in the name of that King. But all the Cardinals of the Spanish faction were prohibited to go to it by that imbassador; to which effect the Cardinal D'Estè was advised by the Duke Savelli, the Emperor's imbassador, that he should not go to that consistory. To whom he answered, that, being they did not confide in him in their meetings, he would do what he thought fit;† and upon this occasion he openly declared himself displeased with the Spaniards, and was made protector for the kingdom of France.‡ Upon which, he put out a manifesto of his reasons why he turned Frenchman, to which the Spaniard answered; and the Cardinal replied to that answer, and removed the Austrian arms from his palace, and set up the King of France's arms in their place, and began much to defend the Barberini, who proferred to resign to him the great abbacy of Nonantola.§ But the Pope said to him one day, "I see, Monsignore, you take great pains to protect the Barberini, and I do not understand your change, that you now defend those to whom you were contrary ; I doubt it is for your own interest, to get the abbacy to which you pretend, but I would have you know, that they may lay it down, but none can take it up without us." To which Cardinal D'Estè answered, that he did it not for any self interest, " But, holy Father, I defend their cause

---

* "Il Cardinale sudetto s'accorse che," &c.

† "Al che esso non volse obbedire, dando per risposta, che si come li Spagnuoli stimavano di poca essenza la sua persona nella loro congregationi, così anco sarebbe stato di poca essenza l'intervento suo nel consistoro, e per ciò non v' intervene," (p. 157). The last words are rendered by Cogan " and therefore he would goe unto it," (p. 97).

‡ " E gli fu procurato il brevetto della protettione delli regni di Francia."

§ "Honantala," in the original, but Nonantola is clearly meant. The original adds, " che si pretendeva dall' Estensi."

because I think it just; but if your Holiness be displeased with my being at Court, I shall withdraw when your Holiness pleaseth;" to which the Pope answered, " God bless you!;" which, in plain terms, is as much as to say, " Go, in God's name." Upon which the Cardinal took coach, and went presently to Modena, his own country; but after a while he returned to Rome, hearing that the Admiral of Casteele was come thither in quality of embassador extraordinary from Spain. That embassador visited * all the Cardinals but Estè, whereupon there was a great falling out between them, and each of them raised men in arms to about 600 persons, and the Pope himself was fain to bring some forces into the city to quell the tumults, in which several men were slain in the streets. The Cardinal, wanting money to pay his soldiers, pawned his jewels to Cardinal Cava † for the sum of 22 thousand crowns, the money he expected out of France not coming in time, and his brother the Duke had supplied him, but not sufficiently. But afterwards peace was made between them by the mediation of several princes.

He is a person of an angelical life, of great splendor, cheerful, affable, courteous, and officious.‡ [The picture is very like him. J. B. 1677.

I have been at Modena, an ancient city of Lombardia, and a colony of the Romans, where Marcus Antonius besieged Brutus; and after that it was ruined by Goths and Lumbards. It is now but a mean city—the Duke's pallace, when I was there, being but a little more than half built. About 20 miles from it is another small city, called Reggio, belonging to the same Duke; there the court of guard stopped me, and searching my portmantle took out all the books, which were about 2 or 3, and twenty small things, which they put in a bag, and carried them and me to the INQUISITION, where I found the Father Inquisitor (a grey friar) very courteous, wondering to see the souldiers bring the books and me to him. He asked me

* "S' era dichiarato di visitare."  † Cueva?
‡ The French ambassador praises Cardinal d'Este very highly. Fol. 51.

whether I could speak Latin. I told him in Latin, yes, but that my pronunciation of it was different, so that by reason of that he might not understand me. He told me that he understood me well enough. I told him again in Latin that I had lived some years in Italy at several times, and that therefore I could speak Italian if he pleased. " No," said he, " I would discourse with you in Latin, that these souldiers that brought you hither may not understand; for," saith he, " we never use to trouble strangers, gentlemen travellers, in this kind, and I do not understand what should make these fellows do it. There is something of malice in it; you have offended somebody or other, and they have put this trick upon you." (I began to suspect our own English Jesuits at Rome might do it.) " However," saith he, " you know that books in Italy may not be sent or carried about without licence from the Inquisition." I told him that I had formerly learned that at Sienna in Toscany, where I was sent for into the Inquisition for sending of 20lbs worth of books from thence to Rome by the carrier, who instead of carrying them to Rome carried them to the Inquisition; but upon the examination the books proved all allowable, and I had a license, the Father Inquisitor excusing me as being a stranger not knowing the custom; but I told him withal that, I being now just newly come over the Alps out of France, there was no Inquisition there to go to. He allowed my just excuse. " However," saith he, " if I should look over the books, and find any of them printed at any heretical city, as Geneva, Amsterdam, Leyden, London, or the like," he must either take the books from me, and let me go, or else he must clap me up while he had time to examine the books. " Therefore," saith he to me, " do you write over a catalogue of them yourself, and if I find no heretical book amongst them I will subscribe a license to them." I assured him there was no such amongst them; however, he would not look in a book, so that I was fain to write him a catalogue, to which he presently subscribed a license, with his name to it, and wished me a good journey.

This dukedom of Modena is about threescore miles long and forty broad. The Duke layeth a claim also to the neighbour marquisate of Ferrare, which the Pope keepeth from him as being fallen to the state of the Church. Our present Dutchess of York is of this family D'Estè, being a Princess as daughter to that Duke. J. B. 1677.]

## XXVIII.

### VINCENTIVS S. EVSTACHII S. R. E. DIACONVS CARD. COSTAGVTVS
### GENVEN. XIII. JVLII, MDCXXXXIII.

He is a nobleman of Genoüa. He was clerk of the chamber, not thinking to come so soon to be Cardinal as he did, because the Court was then full of ancient men of worth; but he may thank the war of the Barberini for his promotion, as well as many others, who else peradventure had never been Cardinals. But Pope Urban VIII., having occasion of money to maintain the war,[*] made many clerks of the chamber Cardinals to get money for their places from other prelates. Thus was Costaguti preferred.[†] But before his rising his father and he lent the chamber great sums of money, and had their security from the 5 millions which Sixtus V. put into the Castle of St. Angelo. [La Statera de' Porporati, [No. liii. p. 231.]

He is splendid, loving,[‡] pleasant, affable, and courteous. Innocent the X.th hath a kindness for him. He is of a comely aspect, very charitable, and seemeth to be of no faction, but is newtral. He is a learned, intelligent man, and may be called the *Golden Cardinal*, for his dignity cost him 3 times more than it is worth. All that know him love him for his good humour.

[I have forgot whether the picture be like him; but his limner, Joseph Testani, seldom faileth in that point. J. B.]

---

* "Perche gli pareva conveniente dar mano alli accumulati thesori riuchiusi sotto la terra à beneficio delli nepoti, e bisogno che aveva," &c.
† Vide art. xxx. [J. B.]  ‡ "Amabile."

## XXIX.

**JOANNES STEPHANUS S. AGATHE S. R. E. DIACONUS CARD. DONGHIUS. EP'US IMOLENSIS. GENUEN. XIII. JULII, MDCXXXXIII.**

<small>La Giusta Statera de' Porporati. [No. lv. p. 236.]</small>

He was a gentleman of Genoüa, and clerk of the chamber, and very rich. After the unfortunate success of Cardinal Spada's negotiation,\* this man was sent by Urban VIII. apostolical nuntio and plenipotentiary into Lumbardy to treat of peace with the Italian princes, where he spent a second clerkship of the chamber without getting any profit at all, but was for it promoted to the purple, with other his fellow-clerks, that their places might be sould to get money. This Cardinal is curious and learned, and doth good service to the Pope. He was sent legate to Ferrare, where in that charge he was much commended for his good managing affairs. He is affable and courteous, being very rich, and a great almsgiver. He spendeth plentifully, not in vain but in profitable and good things. His genius is Spanish, of which he maketh open profession; put up that King's arms over the porch of his pallace, and in the last conclave he left the Barberini and followed the Spanish faction, who have a great esteem of him, his whole family living under that protection.

[The picture is very like him in the face, but cannot show his tallness. I was told at Rome that, when things went contrary to his mind in the conclave, he in a chafe pulled off his cap, and, throwing it angrily upon the ground, stamped upon it, saying, "I would I had half the money that this base cap hath cost me for it; and then let who will take the cap for me!" said he. J. B.]

<small>\* Vide art. ix. [J. B.]</small>

## XXX.

Paulus Aemili⁹ S. Mariae in Cosmedin S. R. E. Diac. Card.
Rondininus Ep'us Assisien. Roman. xiii Julii, mdcxliii.

He is a gentleman of Rome, nephew to the late Cardinal Zachia, who sought to advance himself on the Spanish pretences.* Pope Urban VIII. having reigned 13 years, wherein he had declared himself so much for the French, that the Spanish Cardinals plotted how to depose him, and choose another Pope; to which end, when Urban, for change of air, went to his country pallace at Castel Gandolfo, the Spanish faction had secretly many congregations, with intentions to choose Cardinal Zachia Pope, and to clap up Urban in the Castle St. Angelo, as being uncapable of the government. But their design was discovered to the Pope, who came suddenly and unexpected to Rome, and called a consistory, when, all the Cardinals being met, Urban stood up, and with a loud voice said, "Where is the new Pope, that I may adore him?" which the Spanish hearing, were amazed and half dead to see themselves discovered. At that time the Pope made a bull or decree, that every Cardinal Archbishop, or Bishop, with all other Bishops that had cure of souls, should go and reside at their churches, upon pain of excommunication and deprivation both of dignity and profit. Upon which poor Cardinal Ludovisio, who was cruelly troubled with the gout, was forced to go to his church at Bologna, where, with excessive pain and grief, he soon died almost distracted. And all those that combined against the Pope shortly after died with disgust and vexation, and in particular the Cardinal Zacchia, Rondinino's uncle.

This man was one of the clerks of the chamber, and was promoted with the rest, as the aforesaid Costaguti was,† and because in the time of the Barberinos' war he raised at his own charge a

[margin: La Statera de' Porporati. [No. liv. p. 233.]]

---

* " d' avanzare le sue pretenzione appresso li Spagnuoli."
† Vide art. xxviii. [J. B.]

company of cuirassiers, besides other services done to that family. He is but of middle intelligence, but proud to the highest degree, insomuch that he scorneth to be civil, or to salute any person which is not his peer, and is discourteous to everybody. He hath plenty of the goods of fortune, is of a middle age,* and delighteth himself in all the pleasures that Rome can afford him. [The picture is like him.

In my writing of these lives I could not but observe that Cardinal D'Este, a prince, Cardinal Donghius, in the next former pages, and this Bondininus, were all but Deacons, and yet all of them Bishops; and Cardinal Deacons are often Popes. J. B. 1677.]†

## XXXI.

STEPHANUS TIT. S. LAURENTII IN PANE ET PERNA, S. R. E. PR'B'R CARD. DURATIUS ARCHIEPISCOPUS GENUAE GENUEN. XXVIII NOVEMB. MDCXXXIII.

La Giusta Statera de' Porporati. [No. xxviii. p. 142.]
He is of the new nobility of Genoüa, who made himself a prelate by buying a clerkship of the chamber, and afterwards he bought the place of the general Apostolic Treasurer, but was presently after promoted to be Cardinal. Urban VIII. imployed him in many charges, and, a little before the wars of the Pope with the Princes of Italy, he was sent Legate to Ferrara; but he left the government when Cardinal Antonio came thither to assist him in arms. Afterwards he returned to his archbishoprick of Genoüa, from whence he never parted but to the conclave in the *sede vacante*. He had much difficulty to get that archbishoprick, but Urban resolved that he should have it in despite of his competitors.

* "huomo di bel tempo." Rather, as Cogan translates, one who "loves his pleasure."

† Vide art. lii. [J. B.] The author seems not to have understood that a church which gives its holder the title of Cardinal-deacon may be held by a person who belongs to the episcopal order.

In his legation of Bologna all the citizens will witness his courteous carriage, to the great satisfaction of those people; yet he was not courted much by the nobility. He is a rich Cardinal, as being of Genoüa, who multiply their wealth by trading as merchants. When he was a prelate, he spent a great deal of money in gaming and upon women. He is poreblind, and hath a cast of one eye. He giveth not much alms, is affable with those that have to do with him; but if he be out of humour there is no dealing with him. He faineth to be of the Austrian faction, but is in truth wholly for France. He is not much esteemed at Court.

He may pray with all the reason in the world—*Delicta juventutis meae et ignorantias meas ne memineris, Domine.* There is nobody but he perhaps could have told how to disentangle himself from those many difficulties he met with in his archiepiscopacy, he having upon sundry occasions disobliged the Senate. But I conclude, having news that he died the 10th of July. Il Cardinalismo, p. 118.

[I never saw him but once or twice, when he came to the conclave of the *sede vacante* on the death of Innocent the X<sup>th</sup>, and therefore I have forgot whether the picture be like him. However, Testani, his eminent countryman, hath favoured his squint eye. J. B. 1662.]

## XXXII.

Mar. Ant. tit. S. M. de Pace S. R. E. Presb. Card. Franciottus Lucen. xxviii 9bris, mdcxxxiii.

He is one of the principal gentlemen of the Republic of Lucca in Toscanie. Coming to Rome, he was made a prelate in buying a clerkship of the chamber, and afterward bought the place of auditor; but a few months afterwards he was promoted by Urban the VIII. to be Cardinal, and was made Bishop of Lucca. He was sent Legate to Ravenna, where he was very well esteemed both of the nobility La Statera de' Porporati. [No. xxix. p. 141.]

and people. He cruelly afflicted his own country upon the accoumpt that I shall tell you; which was this:—

The brother to this Cardinal was one of the consistory and governers of this Republic, but was suspected* by the other, that he aimed to get the whole power into his own hands; and upon search of his house were found several prohibited arms amongst others, and his servants always went armed; and the suspicion increased the more because that city is more vigilant than others that anybody should enter it with any arms—no, not so much as with a knife—being very rigorous to chastise the transgressors of that law. Upon which the Cardinal's brother was imprisoned, with some of his servants, who upon examination were more and more found traitors! Wherefore the senators in few days intended to put them to death. The Cardinal finding no other way to save his family from ruin, fled to Pope Urban, and told his tale otherwise than the truth was really—saying that his brother was imprisoned for private malice and hatred that they had to his Eminence, and that those magistrates had accused him of treason only because that some servants of his episcopal pallace were armed. Whereupon the Pope dispatched presently letters to those magistrates, with order to set the Cardinal's brother at liberty, who was guilty, and worthy of death. To which letters the Republic would not obey; upon which the Pope excommunicated and interdicted them, and commanded all the churches to be shut up, and for a long time no divine office was performed. The Republic put out many protests and writings of their reasons, of which they sent copies to all Christian Princes; but all would not do, they being forced to satisfy the Cardinal before the excommunication could be taken off.

He is a wise, experienced man, and very papable,† being beloved in the college. [J. B. 1622.‡ The picture is like him.

I have been often at Lucca, a strong neat little city. The chief

---

\* " scoperto."  † " soggetto papabile, mà non maturo."
‡ Sic MS.

revenue of the territory is your Lucca olives, small and in branches. The city is very ancient, C. Sempronius retiring thither when Hannibal had routed him at Trebbia and Piacenza; this being not only a colony but a municipal city of the Romans. Julius Cæsar wintering here, together with whom Pompey and Crassus made the first triumvirate in this city. The *Volto Santo*, that is, our Saviour's face on a linnen cloth, standeth with magnificence in the cathedral.\* In the church S<sup>ti</sup> Fridianis is the tomb of one of our English Kings, being one of the Richards, as the epitaph rudely speaketh thus:—

"Hic Rex Richardus requiescit scept[r]ifer almus.
Rex fuit Anglorum," etc.

When I went one time to Lucca, this epitaph was so covered with the ornaments of an altar that I could not find it, neither could they tell us of any such King buried there who shewed us the church. But I, being confident it should be there, caused some of the obstacles to be removed, and so found the epitaph, which I had formerly read; and I desired them to take care that that king's memory might not be forgotten amongst them.† J. B.]

## XXXIII.

CAMILLUS TIT. S. PETRI IN MONTE AUREO S. R. E. PRESB<sup>r</sup>.
CARD. ASTOLLIUS ROMANUS. XIX VII BRIS, MDCL.

Il Sign<sup>r</sup> Camillo Astolli was a young gentleman of Rome, of about 27 years old, and brother to the Marques of that name, that  Il Nipotismo, pt. i. l. iii. p. 119.

---

\* The "Volto Santo" (which the author seems, through a defect of memory, to have confounded with the *Veronica*,) is really a wooden crucifix, said to have been carved by St. Nicodemus. "In the Dome, the *Volto Santo*, which (pardon the tradition) was set miraculously on an image of Our Saviour, carved by Nicodemus, His disciple, while the artist was surmising after what form to express that sacred face." (Raymond, p. 265.) See Murray's Handbook of Central Italy, p. 19, ed. 1861.

† This St. Richard is said to have been King of Wessex, to have abdicated his crown, and to have died at Lucca when on his way to Rome in 722. (*Acta Sanctorum*, Feb. 7.) But there is no record of him in the English Chronicles.

had married a niece of Donna Olympia; they were noble, but very low in estate. There was never acted upon the theatre of the Court of Rome so strange a scene as that of this man; the Pope Innocent X[th] laying aside Cardinal Pamphilio, his nephew and Cardinal Padrone, banishing him the Court, and all the rest of his relations, and took this man, a mere stranger to him, and of but ordinary parts, and on the sodaine made him his adoptive nephew, Cardinal, and Padrone, as if he had been the head of the Pamphilian family. He was of a comely aspect, and of a handsome winning carriage, and well enough accomplished for an ordinary prelate; but very ignorant in public affairs, being a mere novice in all negotiations and policy. But he was broth* in by Cardinal Panzirollo, the Pope's chief confident and Secretary of State, who worked him in so far into the Pope's favour that he gave him the name of Pamphilio, and the keys of his closet, to go in and out when he pleased; which may be reckoned among the prodigious effects of fortune.

[Pp. 123-5.] As long as Cardinal Panzirollo lived, Astolli's fortune was prosperous and good, but no sooner had that Cardinal yealded up his last breath, but Astolli began to perceive the decay of his fortune. For Donna Olympia, the Pope's sister and mistress, that had been laid aside, came now in favour again, upon which Astolli was sodenly banished from Rome, and was ordered by the Pope to lay aside the Cardinal Padrone title and the name of nephew, as well as that of Pamphilio, and this severity was, because that he, seeing he was like to fall, took the King of Spain for his patron, discovering to him the Pope's secret councells (with the Cardinal Barberinos, now restored into the Pope's favour and family), about the surprising the kingdom of Naples; the King of Spain, upon Astolli's advice, providing, and stopping all door of entrance.

[I had once letters of commendation from the then Dutchess of Savoy to Cardinal Penzirolly, and received many audiences and courtesies from him; but he died, and I was at his funeral on the

* i. e. brought.

Monte Cavallo, *olim* the Quirinal Hill. At my being since at Rome, I heard that all this business of Astolli's adoption was but a great piece of policy of Pope Innocent, that so Astolli should bear the burthen and the blame of all errors and miscarriages, until that near his death Astolli should be removed, and his true nephew, Prince Pamphilio, should go quietly away with the estate.

When I was last in Italy, 1660, he was in favour at Court, and the Queen of Swethland's *galant*. This picture is very like him. J. B. 1666. Vide art. xxxiv.]

## XXXIV.

### Decius S. Adriani S. R. E. Diaconus Card. Azzolinus Firmanus. ii. Martii, mdcliiii.

Azzolini was a confidant and spy of Donna Olympia's [Pope Innocent the X$^{th}$ sister, that governed both him and the church almost the whole 11 years of his reign.] When Cardinal Astolli * betrays the Pope's councel about the kingdom of Naples unto the Spaniards, this Azzolini took upon him to discover who it was that had betrayed them, and, after exact search, found that it could be nobody but Astolli; whereupon the Pope banished him, and made Azzolini Cardinal for his recompense.† He is of a Sicilian race, though born in the city of Firmo, in the marquisate of Ancona. The course of his exaltation is too long a story. I shall only say that, being conscious of his incapacity of rising to that grandeur his ambition prompted him [to],—as having no means nor merits to advance him, nor anything besides a simple prelature,—he took upon him that way which often taketh at the Court of Rome, and that is, in plain terms, he turned spy; in which he improved himself so well, that it was generally believed there was not any one more dexterous in the discovering the corruptions of others than he,

Il Nipotismo, pt. i, l. iii. p. 125.

* Vide art. xxxiii. [J. B.]      † Cardinalismo, p. 167.

and this he manifested when he smelt out that Cardinal Astalli had discovered to the Spaniards all the Pope's intrigues with the Barberini about the taking of the kingdom of Naples;* for which Astalli was deprived of all that he had, and this man was made Cardinal, and received into favour for his pains. So that hath made the mistery of a spy honourable at the Court of Rome, and others practise it, although not with so good success.†

In the conclave of Rospigliosi he did him so good service, that the very night of his being elected Pope he declared Azzolini Secretary of State. His chiefest part is a dexterity of the pen. But his amours to all kinds of ladies ecclipse all his parts; his poor and abject spirit in that kind yieldeth himself up to certain doxies brought into his chamber by a certain fryer, his pandor. But since he began to have familiar conversation in the Court of the Queen of Sweden, his thoughts are somewhat advanced. Pope Alexander VII. not enduring the publiqueness of this Cardinal's amours, sent him legate to Romania, rather to remove him out of his sight than for anything else.

[The picture is very like him. J. B. 1662.

This Christina, Queen of Sweden, as being the daughter to the great Gustavus Adolphus, and bred up a Protestant in the Lutheran way, quitted her crown and her religion too, turning papist, and was received at Inspruck, in Tiroll, by that Archduke and Prince with extraordinary great pomp and magnificence; that being the appointed place, at the confines of Italy and Germany, for her to renounce her former religion of a Lutheran Protestant, and to be received into the bosom of the Church of Rome;‡ which was done

---

* Vide art. xxxiii. [J. B.]

† The paragraph in the Cardinalismo ends thus: "So honourable, that at present, in hopes of great rewards, there are prelates of greater reputation than he have undertaken the same way."

‡ In the British Museum is a tract of 48 pages, entitled "Festiva Receptio Virginis Christinae, Succorum, Gothorum, Vandalorum Reginæ, in hac celebri Oeniponte, Provinciæ

with great solemnity; at which I was present, staying there a month for that purpose.

Almost all the Emperor's Court and other nobility were there, the Pope, Alexander VII., sending thither as his internuntio Monsig.<sup>r</sup> Lucas Holstenius to receive her renunciation and admitter [admit her?] into the Roman faith. That internuntio was a high German, of Hamburgh, and had been bred up a Lutheran, but turned as she did, and, being a great scholler, he was the keeper of the Vatican Library, and Canon of St. Peter's at Rome, and my former courteous acquaintance; which, with all kindness, he renewed at our meeting here—he giving me 3 sheets of paper printed in Latin of the solemnity, of which she read half an one very readily in a loud, manly voice, undauntedly.* But her carriage in the church was very scandalous—laughing and gigling, and curling and trimming her locks, and motion of her hands and body was so odd that I heard some Italians that were near me say, *E matta, per Dio*, " By God, she is madd!" and, truly, I thought so too, there being in her no sign of devotion, but all was as to her as if she had been at a play, whilst she received the Sacrament in the Roman mode,† and all in time of the short sermon. But she had short sermons all the week after, every day in a several language; all which she under-

---

Tirolis urbe. Ac ejus Publica Fidei Catholicae Professio iii. Novembris labentis anni celebrata in manibus illustriss. et reverendiss. D. D. Lucae Holstenii, delegati sanctissimi Domini nostri Alexandri Papae VII., in Templo aulico, cui Fratres Minores strict. obser. inserviunt. Coram sereniss. Archiducibus, Fernando Carolo, comite Regnante, Anna Medicea, ejus conjuge, ac Sigismundo Francisco, Augustae et Gorcensis episcopi, necnon excellentiss. D. Legato Regis Catholici Antonio de Pimentel et Prado, ad quem haec brevis Narratio mittitur. Oenip. et Bolognae, 1656."

* " Accepit ab eo grande folium, cui Fidei Professio inerat, ac voce mascula et perceptibili . . . . totum legit, distincte adeo atque polite, cum debita pausa omnia verba pronuntiando, ut ex hac lectione peritiam maximam in Latina lingua se habere etiam honeste doctis ostenderit." (Festiva Receptio, p. 15.) " Vox ejus sonum habet clarum, et parum muliebre" [*sic*]. Ib. 25.

† The writer of the Festiva Receptio states (p. 16), that she did not communicate on this occasion, having resolved that her first public reception of the sacrament should be at the Pope's own hands.

stood well, as I was told there by Monsig$^r$ Holstenius, the Pope's internuntio, with whom I was often.

That night she was entertayned with a most excellent opera, all in musick, and in Italian, the actors of that play being all of that nation, and, as some of themselves told me, they were 7 *castrati* or eunuchs; the rest were whoores, monks, fryers, and priests. I am sure it lasted about 6 or 7 hours, with most strangely excellent scenes and ravishing musick,* of all which, by the Archbishop's order, the Sig$^r$ Conte Collhelo † presented me with a book in Italian, which I have now in my study, with all the scenes in excellent brasscutts. The title is " L'ARGIA, Dramma Musicale, reppresentato a INSPRUGG alla maesta della serenissima Christina, Regina di Suezia," &c. She stayed at Insprugg about ten days, and every day had its variety of entertaynement, what in dancing, musick, banquetings, hawking, and hunting all sorts of wild fowls and wild beasts, incompassed in toyles of canvas, making a wall (as it were) with timber, poles, and canvas 5 or 6 miles in compass to bring in the several herds of wild beasts that inhabit that Alpine country, amongst which the *camuccii* or *chamois*, or mountainous wild goats, are most in number; there being culverines and small canons placed here and there for Her Majesty to fire at whole droves or flocks of them as they run and lepped to and again. In short, I was told there by an Englishman of the Archduke's music, that those 10 days cost that prince about 30,000$^{lbs}$ English.

I designed that figure of the Queen myself, and had it cut in brass at Inspruck for me, which I have in my study. J. B. 1662.]‡

---

\* See the Festiva Receptio, pp. 19—21.   † Colloredo?

‡ The plate is not among Dr. Bargrave's collections at Canterbury; but a fac-simile of the impression is given as a frontispiece to this volume.

## XXXV.

ALDERANUS TIT. S. PUDENTIANAE S. R. E. PRESB. CARD. CYBO
EP'US AESINUS DE MASSA CARRARIAE. VI MARTII, MDCXLV.

He was a prelate about 35 years of age, and is son to the Prince of Massa Carara; and, as soon as Cardinal Pamphilio was made Pope, his Holiness declared him maggiordomo or superior of the sacred Apostolic Pallace. And because Cibo's pallace was contiguous to that of his Holiness, Cibo proffered it as a guift; but the Pope refused it upon those terms, yet gave him the value for it, that he might enlarge his own pallace by putting these two into one. Innocent VIII. was of the family of Cibo, who was the original of the greatness of the house of Pamphilio, and therefore, when he was elected Pope, he would be called Innocent the X$^{th}$. [La Giusta Statera de' Porporati. [No. vi. p. 26.]

This young Cardinal is of great integrity and virtue and goodness of life. He retireth himself universally from commerce, not conversing with the prelates when he was a prelate * but upon urgent occasions. He is of a studious life, seldom merry, but is delighted much in musick. The actions of this Cardinal are not subject to any censure, nevertheless I can say, *Nullus homo innocens, sed Deus solus justus et impeccabilis.* Finally, all vice discovereth itself, and every small failing is taken notice of, and his retiredness is to get credit, especially with those that are friends to the house of Austria † He is a devote of the house of Austria, his progenitors living under the protection of that crown. He is beloved not only of the Pope, but of all the sacred college. He hath pretensions to the Popedom, which maketh him live so retiredly.‡ [Supplimento, MS. f. 29. [La Statera, p. 22.]

---

* "Sendo non solo ritirato dall' universal comercio, mà anco da quello dei prelati."

† "E se pur lui è stato ritirato, non è stato per altro che per acquistar credito, e si è conosciuto veramente esser affettionato e divoto di casa d' Austria." This sentence has been transferred from the end of the article.

‡ The French ambassador speaks very highly of Cibo. Fol. 44.

[I have bin at Massa Carara, near the Mediterranean seaside, just beyond the *Ripa* or *Riva* of Genua, where that Prince hath a stately pallace of marble; his chief revenues consisting in the marble quarries of all veins and colours in his little territory at Carrara; which marble mountains are plainly discerned at a short distance from the road.

The picture is very like him. J. B. 1677.]

## XXXVI.

FEDERICUS TIT. S. MARTINI IN MONTIB. S. R. E. PR'BR. CARD. SFORTIA ROMANUS. VI MARTII, MDCXXXV.

*Il Nipotismo, pt. i, l. iii, p. 122.*

Cardinal Sforza always assumeth to himself the liberty of saying of anything, and therefore, as soon as he heard that Pope Innocent the X[th] had made Astolli Cardinal and adopted nephew, he said openly, "Now the future Popes will never fail of nephews, for they will make whole regiments of them, and fill with such a generation our college of Cardinals."

*La Statera de' Porporati. [No. vii, p. 36.]*

He is a nobleman of Rome, about 44 years old, brother to the Duke of that name. He was a prelate, as being one of the protonotaries in the time of Urban VIII., under whom he had no other imploy than to be Vice-Legate at Avignon, sent thither by Cardinal Antonio, the legate, with an intention to have procured him a Cardinalship;* but for some private interesses could not effect it. Innocent the X[th] made him Cardinal at his second promotion, that so great a family might not be without the scarlate; who have been rulers of the Dukedom of Milan, and have had many Cardinals of that house.

He is of a reasonable intelligence, not very rich, and therefore a little miserable. He was, after Cardinal Antonio's flight,† by the

---

\* "Di ritirarlo anco al Cardinalato." † Vide art. xii. [J. B.]

Pope made Vice-Chamberlain of Holy Church. He is a man of a pleasant humour,* loves comedies and feasting, and when he was a prelate he delighted much in conversation. It is thought that his genius and inclination is for the French, for two reasons: the first, for his being legate at Avignon; the second, because the French do much court him.† But he himself seemeth to be neutral;‡ yet most think that upon occasion he would prove Spaniolized, because of the great revenues his brother the Duke hath in the state of Milan—being lately also heir to many castles there by the death of a kinsman. He is no great friend to Cardinal Antonio, because he, putting him in hopes that his uncle Urban VIII. would make him a Cardinal, made him sell him his pallace in the Piazza Sforza in Rome at a very low price--now called Cardinal Antonio's Pallace or Barberino's; and because Antonio gave it to the Queen of France, it is now called the Pallace Royall, where the imbassador of France liveth, or any other prince or nobleman that came from that court. [It is new built, and one of the fairest pallaces of Rome. In the court before it, on the ground, layeth a large piece of an Egyptian obelisc full of hieroglifics.

The picture is very like him. J. B. 1662.]

## XXXVII.

FABRITIUS TIT. S. AUGUSTINI S. R. E. PRESB. CARD. SABELLUS ROMANUS. VII. 8BRIS, MDCXLVII.

He was son to Prince Sabelli, the Emperor's imbassador at Rome. La Statera de' Porporati. He is old, having served in Germany, with the title of General. [No. xi. p. 47.] He was taken several times prisoner by the Switzers. At his last

---

\* " di bel tempo."

† " Per che si è visto di continuo, che lui hà nel suo corteggio gran quantità de Francesi." Sforza is not in favour with the French ambassador. Fol. 53.

‡ " Ma lui si dimostra esser neutrale eccetto del papa."

CAMD. SOC. L

imprisonment* he suborned his guard, and made his escape to Rome, carrying his guard with him, whom he rewarded with an annual large pension and a house to live conveniently.

In the war of Urban the VIII. with the Princes of Italy he was declared General against the Great Duke of Toscany, in which business he carried himself slowly, when he might have endamaged the enemy, but did not, because he saw Urban was old and could not live long, and he had a respect to the Great Duke.† Wherefore he was recalled for from Campania, and Don Tadeo, his Holinesses nephew, was made Generalissimo.

This family, both for its antiquity and nobility, enjoy many privileges, among which one is that in the time of the *Sede vacante* he keepeth the keys of the conclave, and at the charges of the chamber raiseth soldiers for theirs and his guard. He hath power of life and death, not only of mean persons, but of those of quality also, he having sent several to the gallies, and beheaded Sigr. Giulio Donati, auditor to Cardinal Antonio, Lord Chamberlain to the Church, because he went to speak with his patron without leave. The gallows at St. Peter's standeth ready for execution. This family hath had two Popes and an infinite number of Cardinals. The ancient city of Urbano belongeth to that family.

When he was Archbishop of Salerno he was beloved by those people, but at length he grew so to love money that for money he favoured one that had killed 10 men.‡ He is knowing, loving, grateful, but very proud. He is wholly for the House of Austria, and affronted the French imbassador by denying him audience because he had first visited the Spanish imbassador before he came to him.§

[When Sir George Savill, baronet, of Yorksheere, now Lord

---

\* " sendo preggione sotto la parola."

† " per il che gli rendeva poco conto inimicarsi un prencipe potente comm' è quello."

‡ " in modo che per denari aggraccierebbe chi havesse amazzato dieci huomini."

§ " Non è troppo amico dell' ambasciadore di Francia, il quale l' affrontò, negandoli l' audienza per che andava prima dall' ambasciadore di Spagna."

Halifax, was at Rome, this Cardinal made very much of him, calling him cousin, and showed him it was so. The picture is like him. J. B. 1676.]

## XXXVIII.

### CHRISTOPHORUS TIT. SANCTI MARCI S. R. E. PRESB. CARD. VIDMAN VENETUS. VII. OCTOB. MDCXLVII.

He was born at Venice, his forefathers being of low and vile condition. This man's father turned factor to marchants, in which he thrived so well that he grew rich and became a marchant himself, and with it purchased a great estate, buying many castles in Carinthia and Ortenburg. This Christopher came to Rome in the time of Urban VIII., and made himself a prelate by buying a clerkship of the chamber, in which place he showed the talent which God had given him. Afterwards, the auditor of the chamber's place being void, he bought it, paying the usual price. Pope Urban dying, and Cardinal Pamphilio being chosen, by the name of Innocent the X[th], he, according to custom, sold the offices of clerks, auditors, and treasurer, creating the former ones Cardinals; and Vidman came by his purple. [La Giusta Statera de' Porporati. [No. xiii. p. 54.]

He is a proper, personable, lusty, strong man. He and the Conte his brother are of one humour; both of them delighting in gaming, feasting, comedies, and the company of women. They are noble Venetians, having bought that honour at the expense of a hundredth thousand ducats, the price that republick hath set towards the maintaining of the war against the Turk.

This Cardinal is of a very good humour,—loving, cheerful, officious, facetious, curious, and courteous, honouring all that honour him, rendering to every one courtesy for courtesy. He cometh of a German race, and is as splendid as any Venetian.

[I, often using to walk alone the usual walk, and play at pall mall under the very high walls of Rome, between the ancient Porta

Flaminia, now Porta del Popolo, and so by the Muro Torto or Nero's Tomb, to the Porta Pinciana or Collatina, I often met him there several mornings, walking *incognito* (as the term is), that is, as a private man, and with a small retinue, and not as a Cardinal; where I, when he spake to me, was to take no notice of his Eminency. He asking me what countryman I was, and said he thought that he had seen me several times at Rome, I told him that I was an Englishman; that I found him there always courteous to myself and to all strangers; and so he was. The picture is very like him. J. B. 1662.]

## XXXIX.

Jo. Fran. Paul. Gondus tit. S. Mariae supra Minerv. S. R. E. Presb. Card. De Retz nuncupat. Archiep. Paris. Gall⁹. xix. Febr. mdclii.

Il Cardinalismo, p. 159.

He is of the nobility of France, and was promoted to be Cardinal at the instance of the King of France, with whom he was afterwards disgusted, having received some considerable affronts, though he was Archbishop of Paris. The Court cried out exceedingly against Mazarine, who governed all at that time, and was the principal cause of the persecuting this person, and that upon good grounds. The ecclesiastics pretended that the greatest princes that are cannot repress the power of a Cardinal when they are treating of matters of state—no, though the Cardinal be contriving the ruin or disturbance of the publique peace; but this is a doctrine that princes do now but laugh at, especially the Kings of France, who, upon any such occasion, do fly presently to their Gallican rites.*

It was strange to Pope Innocent the X$^{th}$., that, after the Crown of France had with so much instance and importunity recommended

---

* *i. e.* rights.

this person to be promoted, and after he was advanced to so honourable a dignity, he should be so slighted, imprisoned,* and ill-used by the Crown, of which he made frequent complaint to Mazarine,† who wanted not his pretences of excuse. They that understood the spirit of the man, inclined always to distract and perplex the quiet of his superiors, were much scandalized to see Mazarine so endeavour to make him equal in dignity with himself, and by consequence to give him greater opportunity and encouragement to undertake what in effect he did enterprize. But Mazarine was obliged to do what he did for private and occult reasons, not imagining the said person could have been able to have kindled so great a conflagration as he did. The Spaniards endeavoured what they could to fetch over this Cardinal to their party, promising, as is reported, much more than he could hope for in France; but he, that had his aim upon France, kept himself close to the interest of that Crown, demonstrating upon several occasions that his adhering to the male-contents was not from any animosity to that kingdom, but only to humble the fortunes of Cardinal Mazarine. At the time that accident happened to the Duke of Crequy at Rome, which was August 20, 1663, amongst all the Cardinals there was none that stuck so close to the French party as he, to the admiration of everybody—that a person that had been turned out of his archiepiscopal church and other benefices, had been imprisoned, persecuted, and banished, should appear with such ardour in defence of that interest that was the cause of his troubles, and (which was worse,) resolved never to re-admit him to those dignities he had lost. But his proceedings in this point were prudent enough; for, having voluntarily disobliged his Most Christian Majesty,‡ it was but reason he should be voluntarily obliged; and the King of France, willing to let the

---

\* This word is inserted by Bargrave.
† Vide art. xxvi. [J. B.]
‡ "Obligando sua maestà volontariamente, già che volontariamente l' haveva disobligato." (Il Cardinalismo, part ii. p. 212.) *i. e.* although the King had disobliged the Cardinal. Bargrave follows the English translation.

constancy or generosity of Retz, with which he maintained the just privileges of his Crown, to go unrewarded, he admitted him again into his favour, which he enjoys unto this day, but with some conditional limitations, as retaining still in his mind the prejudice he did formerly to the Crown, though he often declared that all his designs were against Mazarine.

[I, that am now a writing of this Cardinal, do not remember that I ever saw him in France, but heard much there of him and the contests he had with Mazarino, and of his being imprisoned at the Bois de Vincennes, and afterwards at Nantes, from whence he made his escape to Belle Isle, at the mouth of the Loyre river, in Britany—that island being his proper inheritance. I heard likewise (and I think read) his geneologi to be of Italy, though he were born a Frenchman. But I remember very well that I was at Rome when, after his escape, he came thither; where in Strada Gregoriana he lay 3 weeks or a month incognito—I being showed the palazzino (or little pallace) several times where he privately lived before it could be contrived fit for him to have audience of the Pope, there being great contests between the Pope and the French King about his imprisonment. All the French then in Rome were likewise either Royalists or Gundeists, there being many times quarrels between the two parties. But at length the Cardinal had his audience, and appeared publicly, all animosities being laid aside. Where I saw him often, and the picture is very like him. Il Conte Gualdo Priorato\* hath written in Italian 10 books of the Revolutions of France, where all the intrigues of Mazarino and Gundi are mentioned; and in his 9th book of Gundi's imprisonment, and the resentiment the Pope had about it. I made an acquaintance with that author at Venice, at the shop where his book in folio is sold, and I bought one, " Appresso Paolo Baglioni, MDCLV." J. B. 1662.]

\* Vide art. xxvi. [J. B.]

## XL.

ALOISIUS TIT. S. ALEXII S. R. E. PRESB. CARD. HOMODEUS
MEDIOLAN. XIX FEB. MDCLII.

From his very first entrance into the prelacy he had an ambitious hankering after a cap, and it cost him and his family no small quantity of money before he did compass his ends. It was thought very strange, his family being like to extinguish for want of heirs, that he would suffer it to perish rather than marry. It is reported that, a friend of his advising him to marry, he replied, " he had higher thoughts." However, things have succeeded to his desires, and that without any disadvantage to his house, which had children afterwards, and is become one of the most conspicuous, richest, and best allied families in Spain. [Il Cardinalismo, p. 159.]

He had first the archbishoprick of Milan given him, which was in his own country, where he was resident for some time, and performed his pastoral functions like a good shepherd, until Innocent the X. made him a Cardinal, a while after discharging himself of his bishoprick, and in good part by means of the Spaniards, who have this for a particular maxim, to make their Cardinals live at Rome as much as possibly they can. And, although he was a Spaniard both in respect of his family and inclinations, yet in the conclave of Innocent, when Alexander VII. was created, he went against the judgment of the Spaniards; but they took not much notice of it, because there were so many concerned in the conspiracy.

This Cardinal is (in short) of a noble extraction, of an exemplary life, and good manners, having shown himself in all congregations and offices a person of much worth, and one that sticks close to the business that belongeth to him. However in his obstinacy he is a little to blame, yet he yields if he be pressed with good words. He is otherwise of a merry disposition, and by the sweetness of his conversation shows that he hath no secret grudge against anybody. For which I would not answer, although he be a good *Lumbard*—which is as much as to say, an enemy to hypocrisy.

He would be no ill Pope, but I much fear he will die a Cardinal; yet not without some hope of the papacy, in which so many of them die. [The picture is very like him—at whose pallace I have often been with an English gentleman of his *seguita* or retinue. J. B. 1662.]

### XLI.

Jo. Hieronymus tit. S. Honuphrii S. R. E. Presb. Card. Lomellinus. Genuen. xix. Feb. mdclii.

[*No account is given of this Cardinal.*]

### XLII.

Jacobus tit. S. Mariae de Transpontina S. R. E. Presb. Card. Corradus Ferrarien. xix. Febr. mdclii.

[*No account given.*]

### XLIII.

Laurentius tit. S. Grysogoni S. R. E. Presb. Card. Imperialis Genuen. xix. Feb. mdclii.

Il Nipotismo, pt. ii. l. ii. pp. 58-59.

This Cardinal Imperiale was Governor of Rome when the French embassador, the Duke of Crequi, received that great affront of having his coach assaulted and fired upon by the Pope's guards. Don Mario, the Pope's brother, engaged him in it before he knew anything of it; yet, nevertheless, he was fain to make a journey into France to justify himself. Yet the French Court shall never forget Cardinal Imperiale, though they are satisfied that the execution only was charged on him unwittingly, plotted by Don Mario. However, upon it the Pope's nuncio was immediately sent away from Paris, and his vice-legate was driven out of Avignon, and the Court of Rome was fain to entertain an army all the time of the treaty, and before, for fear of being surprised by the King's forces; and the agreement was concluded in a dishonourable and shameful way for Rome and for the Church—[a pillar being set up, with an ignominious inscription as to the government;* which stood by the Pope's guards, near the Vatican, for some years, but was † afterwards, upon humble submission and petition to the King of France, it was by his leave taken away, it being not there when I was last at Rome, 1660].

It was a great wonder to many people to see so many persons of much more merit than he past by, and a person made choice of that had done so little service for the Church. But those that looked deeper into the business ceased immediately to wonder, as knowing the riches of his family, and the great ambition they had to have a cap. Nor was that conjunction of time amiss; for Donna Olympia, being again received into favour, designed to re-establish herself by getting of monyes; which is all that can be said for his exaltation. [Il Cardinalismo, p. 160.]

He is of an affable and pleasant nature, and of great frankness and candour in his conversation, and doubtless he would be much more acceptable to all that converse with him, were he not a little too tedious in tracing out other people's thoughts. He in the conclaves is commonly the head of the flying squadron, which giveth no little disgust to the 2 crowns, to see such a combination of Cardinals driving at the destruction of their interest.

The affront he received in his banishment, not only out of the lands of the Church, but out of all Italy, for the insolencies committed by the Pope's guard—the Corsi—upon the Duke and Dutchess of Crequi, the French embassador at Rome, kept him under for awhile, all his judgement and sagacity being too weak to clear him of his accusations, but he was forced to go to Paris and cry *Peccavi!*

[He was Governor at Rome when I was once there. The picture is very like him. J. B. 1662.]

* See Sismondi, Hist. des Français, xv. 58-9.     † *Sic* MS.

## XLIV.

### Gilbertus tit. SS. Joannis et Pauli S. R. E. Presb. Card. Borromeus Mediolanen. xix Febr. mdclii.

*Il Cardinalismo, p. 161.*

This Cardinal, being great-grandchild[*] to Santo Carlo Baromeo, he deporteth himself in all actions modestly, not at all degenerating from those virtues that are natural to that noble family, which hath always given conspicuous examples of their goodness. From the time he took upon him the prelatical habit, he has, in all the offices he has gone through, given great testimonies of his modesty, sincerity, and justice—qualities too rarely visible in persons of that authority and command. In his legation of Romania he behaved himself so well, that there was not the least complaint against him, though some of his court fell into some kind of errors, as having more mind to get money than reputation. However, they abstained from many acts of injustice, for very fear of falling into the legate's displeasure, who they knew was averse to such unequitable designs. In short, the whole court unanimously gives a good account of his sentiments towards the public; yet there wanteth not some criticks that suspect him of some degree of hypocrisy. It is enough he would make a Pope answerable to the desire of the Spaniard—which is, to keep what they have got, and not trouble themselves to acquire whatever is possible, as too many do. But there is no great hopes for him whilst Milan is the Spaniards'; for in the conclave they look not so much upon the merits of the person as the interest of state.

[I have been several times at Milan, where the great St. Ambrose was Bishop; and under the high altar of the church dedicated to his memory is his tomb, supported by four porphyry pillars. 'Tis believed St. Ambrose stood at the gate of this church when he excommunicated Theodosius the Emperor, and would not suffer him to enter in. Hard by is a poor chapel, in a blind corner, with a well,

---

[*] "Pronipote" (pte. ii. p. 219), here meaning *great-nephew*.

where St. Ambrose baptized St. Augustine, as the inscription on
the wall witnesseth:—*Hic Beatus Ambrosius baptizat Augustinum,
Deodatum, et Alippum. Hic Beatus Ambrosius incipit* TE DEUM
LAUDAMUS. *Augustinus sequitur,* TE DOMINUM CONFITEMUR.
But this place is now little regarded; for it is incredible how the
name of S^tus Carolus Boromeus, a Councell of Trent Saint, is so
cried up that St. Ambrose is almost quite neglected.* J. B. 1677.]

## XLV.

MARCELLUS TIT. S. STEPHANI IN MONTE COELIO S. R. E.
PR'BR CARD. SANCTACRUC. EP'US TIBURTIN. ROM. DIE
XIX FEBR. MDCLII.

He is a person that hath added virtue and desert to the nobility [Il Cardinalismo,
of his birth, confirming daily by an hundredth examples the incli- p. 162.
nations that he hath for the publique good; insomuch that in the
congregations and consistories he is one of those that, laying aside
all private passion, devote themselves wholly to the advantage of
the public; and, therefore, many are of an opinion in time there
may be hope for him in the conclave.† The principal reasons that
made Innocent X^th promote him were two—a general and a particular; the general reason was, because the Pope had taken a
resolution to re-advance all the noble families in Rome that began
to lessen and decay in their splendour, that thereby he might render
the city more pompous and majestick. But whether he was induced
to this out of pure generosity, or out of an ambition he had to
oblige all those re-invigorated families to his own, I cannot tell;
be it one or the other, the design was noble, and had been executed

---

\* This paragraph is repeated, with little variation, from Raymond's *Mercurio Italiano*,
pp. 211-2. The inscription on the little chapel is now somewhat different.

† " Vi sarà non poco da sperar per lui in qualche conclave." (Pte. 2, p. 220.) " There
will be great hopes for him in the conclave." (Engl. translation.)

more exactly, had not the importunity of his sister * diverted him, and forced him to sell that which he pretended to give. The particular was, that, several occasions being given to Santa Croce to defend and represent to his Holiness certain intricate and difficult points, he did it with that plainness and facility, it made such an impression in the genius of the Pope, that he thought him worthy of a cap, and declared many times before certain of his Cardinals, that he never gave sentence with less injury to his conscience than after he had consulted and been well informed by Santa Croce. And yet Innocent was esteemed a good lawyer, as he was indeed, yet his understanding was but dull and obtuse, and therefore he loved them best that could make things most easy and perspicuous to his capacity; this I know, he was much commended for promoting this man.

[I have forgot him so far as that I cannot say the picture is like him or not. J. B. 1677.]

## XLVI.

BACCIUS TIT. SS. NEREI ET ACCHILLEI S. R. E. PRESB. CARD. ALDOBRANDINUS FLORENTINUS. XIX. FEB. MDCLII.

[*No account given.*]

## XLVII.

JO. BAT. SPADA TIT. S. SUSA'NAE S. R. E. PRESB. CARD. S. SUSA'NAE NUNCUPATUS LUCEN. II. MARTII, MDCLIIII.

Il Cardinalismo, p. 163.

He was in his prelacy intrusted by Urban VIII. with certain of great and considerable offices, which he discharged to his commendations; yet, though Urban promised him a cap, he was not so good as his word. But Innocent X., being informed of the excellency of his qualities, that the services that he had done to the

* "cousin." (Engl. translation.) "le cantilene della cognata." (Pt. 2, p. 222.)

public might remain unrewarded no longer, he created him Cardinal on the day [and] in the year under written. [March 2, 1654.]

He is a person of great prudence, of a good humour, skilled well enough in the law, and of no small experience in the Court. Cardinal Barberino, that loveth him at the heart, cries him up for one of the greatest politicians in the world, and adds many things more than that to his commendations. The Spaniards have great confidence in him, as looking upon him of a quiet nature, and not given to novelties. But his being so strangely united in affection with Barberino has given the Grand Duke occasion of jealousy, and so much the more because they have espoused the interest of their country.

In his legation of Ferrara he was a little faulty, but they were rather of omission than of commission, he leaving the reins too loose to his ministers to be corrupt, insomuch that they who had any business in his tribunal complained of the rapacity of his officers, and the too great goodness of the Cardinal.

[I have forgot him so far as that I cannot say the picture is or is not like him. J. B. 1677.]

## XLVIII.

PROSPER TIT. S. CALLIXTI S. R. E. PRESB. CARD. CAFFARELLUS ROM. II. MARTII, MDCLIIII.

[*No account given.*]

## XLIX.

FRANCISCUS TIT. S. MARIAE IN VIA S. R. E. PRAESBR.* CARD. ALBIZIUS CAESENATEN. II MARTII, MDCLIV.

He is a well deserving and well affected servant to the Duke of Toscany, whose vassal he is originally, though [he] was born in

* Sic.

Cesena, where, having exercised his pragmatical humour some time, and according to the usual impetuosity of his nature, he constrained a gentleman of that country to handle him like a vassaile indeed; and after such an affront not being able to stay in those parts, he came to Rome, and entered himself in the family of Cardinal Panzirolo, who carried him along with him into Spain, in spight of several of his court that were unwilling to have associated with so extravagant a brain. At his return from Spain he was imployed by Innocent the X[th] in the business of the Jansenists, which he transacted so well that he was looked upon as a person of great abilities and cunning—if for no other reason, for complying so exquisitely with the humour of the Pope, that [he] made him a Cardinal; but the principal cause that some will have of his promotion was the known animosity betwixt him and Cardinal Maculano, a person exceeding odious to Donna Olympia, and the whole house of Pamphilio.* So that it may be said that he was not advanced upon the score of his merits, but that he might be an impediment to all such practices as should be used in favour of the same Maculano.

 The tongue of this Cardinal is extremely satirical, and is many times unsufferably sharp. He hath utterly disobliged the Chigi with his talking; but he reckoneth that a virtue in himself, as being naturally against the corruptions of the age, and therefore he cannot content himself to reprehend vices at private meetings, but in his publique orations he takes delight to ostentate his eloquence in that manner, censuring others without any respect, who is not without faults himself. This satyrical way of proceeding obscures the lustre of his learning and the great experience he has in affairs of the world. For other things he hath a very good head, and is therefore hated by the Spaniard, who is always jealous of such persons as that by their contrivances are able to disturb the repose of the whole universe. [The picture is very like him.

* Vide art. xix. [J. B.]

I have bin at Cesena, within 3 miles of the small but famous river Rubicon, now called Pisatello, towards Faenza and Ravenna. J. B. 1662.]

L.

OCTAVIUS TIT. S. CAECILIAE S. R. E. PRESB. CARD. DE AQUA-
VIVA NEAPOLIT. 11 MARTII, MDCLIV.

He hath a general applause, as a person that hath virtue sufficient to render him worthy of that honour, besides that the nobility of his birth makes him as illustrious as his virtues. He is very well practised in the politics of the Court, and indeed so much, he needs no addition to qualify him for the congregations or other offices. He retains much of the Neapolitan still, though he hath been a long time out of his country; that is, he is liberal of his tongue, but sparing of his purse. Not that he does no generous actions, but only he wanteth the judgment to distribute them with discretion, giving all sometimes to one, and to another nothing, and commonly offers more than he can give, and giveth less than he promiseth.

I know not whether Pope Innocent or Donna Olympia gave him the cap. This lady was able to eradicate from the Pope's heart the person he affected, and plant her own there. But that which gave the greatest occasion of wonder to the Court was, to see that lady, that was wont to regard nothing but money, should now prefer a person of worth without a feeling in her hand; but many believe his generosity left not [so] great a benefit unrewarded. But, be it as it will, this is most certain, that upon the bare scoare of the cap there was not the least present made; but what might be done on another scoare I know not. For this I am sure of, he knew so well the worth of his family that he had rather be without a cap than to have tainted it with the least thought of simony.

The Spaniards love him and honour him, but I know not whether they be thoroughly satisfied with him, because in many things he

*Il Cardinalismo, p. 164.*

behaves himself like a newter, not shewing the zeal he ought to have, as he is subject to that crown; besides, in the conclave he gave them no perfect content.

[His humour is always to wear his cap in that fashion,* on one side or other, half on, half off. I have often seen him with his cap still at one side or other, as if he were careful it should not stand right, so that he and his cap and picture are very like. J. B. 1662.]

## LI.

JOANNES CAROLUS MEDICES S. GEORGII IN VELABRO S. R. E. DIAC. CARD. JO'ES CAROLUS NUNCUPATUS FLORENT. XIIII. NOVEMB. MDCXLIV.

*La Giusta Statera de' Porporati. [No. lxi. p. 248.]*

This prince is brother to the Great Duke of Toscany, and nephew to the Cardinal of that title.† He was promoted by Innocent the X[th] at the first promotion, together with his Holinesses nephew, at the instance of the Great Duke and of that nephew. He is a prince of no small knowledge, and an expert souldier, but rather by sea than land, he having for some time had the charge of generalissimo by sea with the arms of the King of Spain; he being always most devoted to the House of Austria, as all the rest of that family is, his Catholick Majesty being their protector.

He is a man of some years, but loves the ladies somewhat too much. He is by nature covetous, and not much splendid.‡ The family of the Medici are no great friends to the family of the Barberini, for several reasons, especially for the war they made against those princes, as all the world knoweth.

[I have often seen him at Rome and Florence, and am sure no picture can be liker him than this. J. B. 1662.

His nephew the Prince of Toscany I have often seen, with his

---

\* *i. e.* as represented in the engraving.   † Vide art. iv. [J. B.]
‡ The original describes him as "amorevole e splendido." P. 249.

father the Grand Duke of Florence, when he was a boy. And since he was married he travelled into Spain, France, Germany, England, etc.;* and at London, by the means of Sir Barnard Gascon, a Florentine of my old acquaintance, I had audience of him and an houre's discourse, he telling me that he remembered that he had often seen me at Florence, and asked me many things about my travels, and told me how much he himself was pleased with his travels, adding many compliments as to England and his obligations to that Court. He is a short, thick man, with a very black hare † and great leggs; a man of excellent parts and great experience, and now succeedeth his father in the Grand Dukedom of Toscany.

I remember that one of the times that I was at Florence, in the Great Duke's most famous gallery, I found Cromwell's picture hanged up amongst the heroes (which vexed me); and I, after a day or two, having audience of the Great Duke (father to the present), he asked me how long it was since I was there last. I told him about 5 years. "Then," said he, "I have added much to my gallery since you saw it last." To which I answered, that there was one picture added, which was Cromwell's, that spoyled all the rest. At which he stopped, and did not know well how to take it; but, at length, said he, "On occasion it is as easily taken down as it was hanged up." J. B. 1679.]

## LII.

BENEDICTUS SS. COSMAE ET DAMIANI S. R. E. DIAC. CARD.
ODESCALCHUS COMENSIS. VI. MARTII, MDCXLV.

[The author is owt in saying that he is a nobleman of Milan city,‡ La Giusta Statera de' seeing that under his picture he is said to be of the city of Como, in Porporati, the dukedom of Milan, which layeth at the end of a great long lake, [No. x. p. 42.]

---

* An account of the Travels of Cosmo III., by Magalotti, was published in an English translation, London, 1821. There is a copy of the Italian MS. (which has never been printed) in the Grenville Library (British Museum).

† Sic MS.   ‡ "Nobile della città di Milano."

in the Romans' time called *Lacus Larius*, now Lago di Como, in Lombardy; into which runneth the river of Adda, through the Valtoline among the Grisons. Those that go into Italy over the Alps this way must pass the Mount Splugen to Chiavenna, the key into Italy, down this lake, and so by Como to Milan. By his birth at Como, of a noble race, he is subject to the King of Spain, and of the faction (the Italians' usual expression) of the House of Austria.] He was about 45 years of age when he was made Cardinal. He courted a long time the Barberini (nephews to Urban the VIII.) to be made clerk of the apostolick chamber, he being very rich [and that a vendable honour]. But, though he had paid his money, the Pope died, and he mist the place. Then, Innocent the $X^{th}$ being chosen, he courted much Donna Olympia, the Pope's sister-in-law [that then ruled all], giving her, amongst other things, a cabinet of plate, which a goldsmith told him that she had a mind to, but was lought* to pay the money, which was 8000 crowns; which money he paid the goldsmith, and sent it her for a present, and she rewarded him with a Cardinal's cap.†

He is a man of a middle intelligence, and, although he hath binn at great expense, yet he is a rich Cardinal—very splendid and affable, having a great kindness for the family of Pamphilio. In the time of his prelature, as clerk of the apostolick chamber, he was much given to passtimes, comedies, banquetines, and feasts; but since he has bin Cardinal he is much retired, and avoideth

* *i. e.* loth.
† " Essendo andato nelli principii dell' assuntione d'Innocentio X., alla casa della su Donna Olimpia un' orefice per mostrarli una bellissima credenza d'argenteria da vendersi, e havendo la detta signora molto ben riguardato, ritrovandosi presente il detto Odeschalchi con altri signori, intesero che detta signora rispondesse che detta argenteria era bella, mà che lei era povera vedova, per la qual cosa non poteva far quella spesa, e detto questo sene entra in camera; all' hora Odeschalchi, chiamato quell' orefice dell' argenteria, gli domandò della spesa di quella, e convenutisi frà loro la pagò 8000 scudi, poi senza dir altro la fece presentare alla detta Donna Olimpia, quale visto si nobil dono, rimasi fuor di se medesima della maraviglia, e andata seno al Papa, gli domandò in gracia per questo soggetto il chiericato di camera, e poi anco la porpora."

common commerce and conversation. [He was, 1676, chosen Pope, and, as I heard, by the name of Innocent the XI^th.

I, having binn 4 times from London at Rome, have seen him very many times, and can assure you that this picture is extraordinarily like him. And as for the lady Donna Olympia, his patroness, she governed the Roman court and chair almost all her brother Pope Innocent the X^th's time, about 10 years; and I had the honour (if it were an honour), upon an occasion of a kind of tumultuous popular clamour against her, in the great court of the Vatican, to hand her from her coach, and make way for her to the door she was to enter, for which she thanked me.

I have seen afar off, not the city but the great lake of Como, at the foot of the Alps, as I went from Milan. J. B. 1677.]

## LIII.

NICOLAUS TIT. S. MARIE ANGELORU' S. R. S. PRESBIT. CARD. LUDOVISIUS MAIOR PENITENTIARIUS BONONI'. VI. MARTII, MDCXXXXV.

This lord obtained his cap by fortune merely, his merits not ren- dering him worthy of that honour, though he was indued with judgement and other qualities good enough for a prelate. The archbishoprick of Bolonia was not conferred upon him in considera- tion of his merits, so much as of the pensions that were upon it. His nephews,* out of an ambition of having an archbishoprick at their devotion in their own country, encouraged him to take it, though little worth, and so he did. The Prince Ludovisi being about this time married to a neece of Pope Innocent's X^th, this man was consequently introduced into the favour of the said Pope, though but indifferently, because Donna Olympia had no hand in it. The Prince began to imagine it would be convenient to have a Cardinal

*Il Cardinalismo, p. 153.*

---

* "Li parenti." (Pte. ii. p. 190.)

of his own family, that he might have the better intelligence of the secrets of the Court; and, ruminating with himself of this and of that, the archbishop came at last into his mind, who was his cousin by the mother's side, and carried the name of Nicolo Albergati; so that he intreated his Holiness to confer a cap upon the said Albergati, but upon condition he should renounce the name of Albergati, and be called Cardinal Ludovisi. His Holiness satisfied the desire of the Prince, with the conditions proposed, and Albergati made no difficulty to accept them, and take upon himself the name of Ludovisi and the cardinalship together. And these were the degrees by which this person ascended to the purple, the Prince defraying all the expenses, as if he had been his own brother.

The Pope, having an eye upon his indigence, made him chief penitentiary, and sent him apostolic legate to Florence to christen a son of the Great Duke. In which legation he was presented with very fine arras hangings and other curiosities for his chamber, the Grand Duke very well understanding what he had principally need of.

Many believe he may raise his fortunes in some conclave or other, his exemplariness of life and the good reputation of all his kindred, and the great affection the Spaniards bear him, making much for it. And he takes glory to espouse the Spanish interest.*

[The picture is like him. J. B. 1662.]

## LIV.

LAURENTIUS SANC. ANGELI IN FORO PISCIUM S. R. E. DIACONUS
CARD. RAGGIUS. GENUEN. VII. OCTOB. MDCXLVII.

La Giusta Statera de' Porporati. [No. xiv. p. 57.]

A nobleman of the new nobility of Genoüa, nephew to the deceased Cardinal of the same name; which defunct in the time of

* The French ambassador says, "Per se non val niente, mà val assai per rispetto del principe suo cugino ... è buon huomo e senza malitia." Vol. 44.

Urban VIII. was made * clerk and auditor of the chamber. He was not only a very simple man, but very ignorant of all human learning; which was known to every body, so that he meddled not much in affairs, but gave the accustomed audiences for formality. His ignorance was grossly known on all occasions, and, in particular, when a prior informed him in a cause which a proctor endeavoured to defend,† the auditor Raggi adhering to the contrary part, the proctor demonstrating to him the clear reasons of his principles with vigour, alleging many authors ‡ in behalf of his principles, and, in particular, the *codex* of the law in such a law.§ The auditor, thinking the *codex* to be a witness, a man, to be ready to assert the truth, spake alowd to the proctor, saying "Codex [is a knave, and] I'll chastise him!" asking where he dwelt, for he would imprison him and send him to the gallies. The proctor tould him he was to be found at the advocate's house; upon which Raggi called for a publick notary, and gave him order to cause a serjeant at arms‖ to go to the advocate's house and arrest Codex and bring him to him. Which was done accordingly, and the advocate delivered the book *Codex* to the officers—some thinking it was some [heretical] prohibited book, and was therefore carried before Monsigr Raggi. The proctor opened the book, and showed him the law by which he pleaded. Raggi, the auditor, stood amazed, like a statue, being, as it were, out of his wits, especially when the comediants made plays upon it, and Pope Urban ¶ could not but laugh at his simplicity.

Divers other such stories of his silliness go about Rome. Before he was Cardinal he made himself Cardinal's clothes, and, putting

---

* " Comprando."
† " Il procuratore desiderava diffendere."
‡ " Cominciò à dimostrare le vive raggioni che la sua parte principalmente teneva sua quella causa [,] in vigore di che allegava molti auttori."
§ " Che il Codice nella legge tale apertamente diceva il detto prencipale."
‖ " Li sbirri."
¶ " E per le comedie che sene fecero per la città di questo fatto, ne fu data parte all santita di Urbano VIII."

them sometimes on, would call his servants to him,* and ask them whether they became him, and whether he was grave enough, and the like. One day he went to the Pope, and said, " Holy Father, made [make] me a Cardinal before my father dieth, that both you and I may pleasure the old man before his death." And when he was made a Cardinal, he † [instead of kissing the Pope's slipper] he ran to him, and hugged him, and imbraced him, and kissed him on both cheeks, saying, " I will hugg ye and buss ye, that I will, for joy that you have made me a Cardinal!" And the Pope [was pleased to laugh at him heartily, he] loving his simplicity.‡ And for his sake he made this Laurenzo his nevew treasorer in the uncle's place; to whom the simple uncle said, " Hark you, nevew, if you mean to come to this honour that I am come to, you must take pains, and study as I have done;" at which both [the Pope and] the nevew and the whole company laughed heartily.

In the time of Barbarinian warr, there were great gabells and imposts all over the state of the Church, and yet the souldiers were not well paid, but were often tumultuous; so that, Urban VIII. dying, and Innocent the X$^{th}$ being chosen, the second day after his election he ordered this treasurer Raggi to make 4 payments § to those souldiers that guarded the conclave, and to disband them. But he paid them but two; at which they in disdain tumultuously set upon the barch ‖ where the money was, and sackaged all, and every one took what he could, Raggi flying for his life, and Don Tadeo, the last Pope's nephew, was fain to hide himself, the souldiers bringing two pieces of canon to besiege his pallace. ¶ But Pope Innocent, with his wisdom and prudence, then new elected, put a

* " E passeggiando chiamava i suoi famigliari della Corte."
† Sic MS.
‡ " Giustava tanto il Pontefice Urbano Ottavo di questo huomo, che non si puol dir più."
§ " Paghe," i. e. so many months' pay. (Cogan's translation.)
‖ " La barcha," probably a misprint for " lancha." The Vocab. della Crusca defines *bancu* as meaning a place where soldiers are paid.
¶ " Per gettar à terra le porte."

remedy to all, and satisfied the souldiery, but was very angry with Raggius, sending to him to lay down his office of treasurership; but afterwards, by the mediation of friends, it went no further, and a while after he was promoted Cardinal.

He is young, being but 25 years old. He is of good conversation, but ambitious and covetous. He is neither learned nor ignorant, but may pass in the way of mediocrity.* [The picture is somewhat, but not very, like him. J. B. 1662.]

## LV.

FRANCISCUS S. M IN PORTICU, S. R. E. DIACONUS CARD. MAIDALCHINUS† VITERBIEN. VII. VIIIBRIS, MDCIIII.‡

He was born at Viterbo, nephew to Donna Olympia Maidalchini, sister-in-law to Pope Innocent the X$^{th}$. He was a destituted young lad, out of all conversation, and of mien or look not like others,— untractable, rude, uncivil,§—and went to school not only to learn to read, but to learn manners. So soon as Innocent the X$^{th}$ was Pope, his aunt got him to be an abbot; with which he lived privately out of the way. About that time Don Camillo Pamphilio, son to Donna Olympia and nephew to the Pope, was promoted to be a Cardinal. It fortuned that Don Paolo Borghese, a prince, died, and so left his wife the Princess Olympia Aldobrandini Rossana a widow, with whom Cardinal Pamphilio, the Pope's only nephew, fell in love, and, unknown (as was pretended) to his uncle the Pope, married her, quitting his Cardinal's cap and nepotism; upon which he and his princess were banished the Court *pro forma*. But Donna Olympia indeavoured what she could to have placed this silly, iddiotly, coxcombly Cardinal Maidalchino to have been Cardinal

La Giusta Statera de' Porporati. [No. xv. p. 66.]

---

* The French ambassador says, " Raggi ha spirito grande, e à mio credere è di più alti ingegni che siano hoggi alla Corte di Roma." Fol. 55.
† The variety of ways in which this name is written will be noticed.
‡ *i.e.* 1647.
§ " Perche la vista non ha in sè vivacità di trattare con civiltà."

Padrone, and Chief Governor of the Catholic Church. But the Pope's own sisters, that were nuns, and other his religious relations, came upon bended knees and [with] weeping eyes,* to beseech his Holiness not to give a scandal to the Church, saying it was a shame already that he was a Cardinal, and a great disgrace to the whole College; and they prevailed with the Pope to lay aside Donna Olympia's designs for her simple nephew.

He is a person so ignorant that he can scarcely speak; and the other Cardinals do but make him their scoffing-stock to laugh at. By his aunt Donna Olympia's means he was promoted to the cap; to the wonder not only of the court but of all Christendom. The Pope refused her request about half a year, looking upon him as a monster in nature [and a coxcomb (as he is)]; and yet at length he yielded to Donna Olympia, and made him Cardinal,—not full eighteen years of age.† And his aunt Donna Olympia did all that she could to make him Cardinal Padrone, that is, to have governed the whole Roman church under the Pope, as the Barberini did under Urban the VIII. But Pope Innocent had great regret that he had made him a Cardinal; and when Alexander the VII. succeeded Innocent the X., he banished Maldachino the court, and sent him a great distance from Rome, but upon request of the rest of the Cardinals he was set at liberty. He first espoused the interest of Spain; but, finding the Spaniards not esteem him, he turned to the French, whereupon the Spaniards stopped all his revenues of several abbacies that he had in that king's dominions; so that on one morning he resigned these abbacies into the Pope's hands, who disposed of them as he thought fit. But the King of France provided otherwise for him.

[I, that am now a-writing, was, 1647, at Rome, when this Car-

*Il Cardinalismo, p. 157.*

---

* "furiosamente e con gran risentimento." (P. 71.) This whole paragraph is much abridged.

† " Commandando 'l Signor Iddio nella legge anticha che li successori d'Aaron fossero sacerdoti per discendenza, può in qualche modo scusarsi 'l Papa d'haver promosso Maldachino parente." (Estampes-Valençay, fol. 55 b.)

dinal was promoted, and I protest he was then, before he had a beard, much more like a monckey or babboone than like a man; so that at St. \* holyday, he coming into S<sup>to</sup> Carlo's Church, in the Curso at Rome, all the women could not hold, but burst out a-laughing at the very sight of him; and he, on the other side, could not hold, but burst out a-laughing aloud too. Amongst many passages of his simplicity daily spoken of, as being within an inch of an idiot, I shall mention but two.

The one is, that he used to go into booksellers' shops, and there, taking down the finest gilded books, and opening them, would seem to be very serious in reading them, whereas he could scarce write or read, as I heard often at Rome; one day, a gentleman of his *sequità* (or retinue), seeing him very earnest at his book, had a mind to see what book it was, and so, looking him over the shoulder, he found that he held the wrong side of the book upwards, with the letters upside down, so that he could not but tell him of it, in way of officiousness. But the Cardinal was very angry with him, and said, "What have you to do which way I have a mind to read; may not I read which way I please, for all you?" The gentleman begged his pardon. "Then" said he, "you should have taken no notice of it at all, or else you should have told it me sooner;" which the gentleman promised to do another time.

The second thing was when I was at Rome, that two persons of quality, his young camerades, carried him to a courtizan's or whore-house, where, being frolic and merry, they fell a-gaming, to cards and dice; and when they had won all the Cardinal's money, then the humour was, that the courtizan and the Cardinal should play for one another's clothes, piece by piece; and so they changed clothes, as one another won and lost, until at last the courtizan or whoore had all the Cardinal's clothes on, and the Cardinal had all the courtizan's. Being thus attired, the humour was, in the dusk of the evening, to go to such and such an one's house, to see

* A blank in MS.

whether they would know him; so into the coach they went, and when they had made a turn or two in the streets, they pretended to have need to make water, so all three went against a wall; but presently my gallants whipt into the coach and drove away, leaving Maldachino alone in the whoore's habit, until at length the watch took him, and used him as a whore in words and language, until that he told them that he was one of Cardinal Maldachinio's mistresses, and he should know all how they used her, upon which they used him the worse for scandalizing a Cardinal, and carried him to the prison door, where he turned off his head clothes, and said, *Son io! Son io!* It is I! It is I! Withat the watch bowed to his eminence, and cried him mercy, and they conducted him to his palace.

When he came to wear a beard he looked more like a man and the picture. J. B. 1662.]

## LVI.

FRIDERICUS SANC. MARIAE NOVAE S. R. E. DIACONUS CARD. DE HASSIA GERMANUS. XIX FEBR. MDCLII.

Il Cardinalismo, p. 162.

He is a person of spirit and generosity, suitable to the nobleness of his extraction. He is very just and exact in his judgement, distinguishing between good and bad to a hair. So it may be said with reason his commendations is * without flattery, his reprehensions without envy, because his praises or rebukes (void of all passion) are proportioned to the merits of the party.

He was translated from the camp to the cloister, from the sword to the cross, from the Protestant religion to the Catholick; which, at the beginning of his promotion, made several persons believe that he would gain but little honour by the Cardinalship—supposing that he had imbibed too much of the confused principles of Protestant and souldier. But they were undeceived when they saw him

* See MS.

give such testimonies of himself that he was expressly a good Catholick and a true observer of the maxims of the Court of Rome. However, the general opinion is that his talent would have been better imployed in matter of arms than the gown, which seemeth to be something forced and unnatural to him, because imposed, and not generated with him, whereas this inclination to arms was born with him,* and he hath retained it from his cradle. The being without (or at least not over well furnished with) the ornaments of learning, which do oftentimes work upon the hearts of the Popes to confer subsidies extraordinary upon such Cardinals as are foreign, is the reason that he wants more conveniences than he injoys, every-one withdrawing himself from his supply, because that to relic him according to the largeness of his own thoughts would require too much. The Spaniards themselves, whose maxim is to inlarge their hands to persons of that quality, have been close enough as to him, because they see that to maintain him in his original grandeur would ask as much as would maintain six others. So that, failing in assignments that were promised him and not paid, he was forced to retire into Germany. The truth is, when he is in Germany, his inclinations are for Rome, and when he is at Rome his inclinations are for Germany.

[The picture is very like him. His family, of the several Landgraves of Hessen, are zealous Protestants; as the confederacy of Smalcald witnesseth. J. B. 1677.]

## LVII.

### CAROLUS BARBERINUS S. R. E. DIAC. CARD. S. CAESARII ROMANUS. XXIII JUNIJ, MDCLIII.

He is the third of that family all at a time Cardinals—never known before, or scarce will be ever again. He is very obsequious  Il Nipotismo, pt. i. l. iii. p. 106.

---

* The words " Whereas ...... with him," are restored from the printed book, as being necessary to the sense.

to his uncle Francesco,* who doth with a great deal of care give him such instructions as may breed virtue and piety in him.

[I remember, when I was first at Rome, an° D<sup>ni</sup> 1646, I by sight judged him to be some 20 years of age. He was looked upon as a youth of great hopes, both as to piety and learning. Many thought that most of his good qualities were feigned, but for my own part I thought I ought to judge well of exterior probity, and leave the secret of dissimulation to Him only that knoweth the heart; though it was said that he was Cardinal Antonio† within, and Cardinal Francesco‡ without.§ I was told at Rome that he had a Scotchman that read Latin, logick, and philosophy to him, after he was Cardinal, when I was there. J. B. 1662.]

‖ Cardinalism o. p. 163.

Pope Innocent the X<sup>th</sup> looked upon it as matter of great importance to destroy, or at the least to abase, the family of the Barberini; but the reconciliation was brought about by means of an alliance contrived by Donna Olympia; who, foreseeing the death of the Pope, sought to make friends, and so resolved something extraordinary, and that was, to negotiate that alliance; and the Princess her daughter that was married to the Prince Justinian having at that time a daughter that was marriageable, she entered into treaty with Cardinal Francesco Barberino for the Prince di Palestrina his nephew, and promised restitution of whatever had been sequestered from them. But they told her that he was inclined to take the prelacy upon him (which was as much as to say he desired a cap). So the Prince Charles resigned his primogeniture to Maffeo Barberino, his younger brother, who married Donna Olympia's great-child,‖ and this Carlo was created Cardinal in respect of the said match, although he had two uncles of his name Cardinals before.

His modesty is so conspicuous and his life so unblamable that he constrains the very enemies of his family to love him, and draws

---

\* Vide art. vii. [J. B.]     † Vide art. xii. [J. B.]
‡ Vide art. vii. [J. B.]     § This is from the Nipotismo, l. 1.
‖ Indistinctly written.

respect from every person in the Court. His obedience to his uncle Francesco appears little less than adoration. He is much in study, devotion, or other spiritual exercises.

[The picture is very like him. J. B. 1677.]

## LVIII.

CAROLUS S. MARIAE IN DOMNICA S. R. E. DIACONUS CARD. PIUS EPISCOPUS FERRARIAE FERRARIEN. II. MARTII, MDCLIV.

Nephew to the lately deceased Cardinal of that name, who by his ill life left no great advantage to his reputation. This man was Treasurer of the Chamber, an office that cost eighty thousand crowns; and he was advanced, as many are, not by his merits but by his money. However, he did well to come by it as he did, otherwise he might have gone without it as long as he lives. Innocent the X$^{th}$ decaying daily, Donna Olympia was still at his elbow, soliciting him perpetually to draw monies to her coffer by selling the Treasurer's place to another. The family of this lord, for its nobility and deserts, might well have deserved a cap without this manner of dealing; but it must be as it may be. [Il Cardinalismo, p. 165.]

He never injoyed his health perfectly from his youth. He had the Church of Ferrara given him in consideration rather of his family than his person; but it would have been better for him to have refused it, and continued at Rome. But he had imbibed the maxim, that the less the Cardinal is present at the Courte, with the more ease will he in time arrive at the papacy. But the politick Romans have by experience taught them another lesson, and he changed his principles too, under pretence that the air of Rome was agreeable to his health.

While he was at Ferrara he was excessively severe, and would fain have reformed all the clergy in his diocess, upon the mere authority of a bishop—doing all not by exhortation but by commination and threatenings,* but found it was too hard to do; for, when zeal is not accompanied with moral prudence to moderate the impulses of nature, it becometh odious even to good men, and, instead of zeal, discovereth itself to be tyranny. And of this sort is the zeal of this Cardinal, who, to speak truth, has but few frailties to correct—either that his infirmities do debilitate his nature or his virtue overpower it.† He is but little inclined to do kindness for any body, and he is too fierce in confutation of him that refuses to yield at the first dash—especially if it be in matter of conscience, in which he is scrupulous to the highest. But this I know, that many persons inferior to him have leapd into the Vatican.

[I cannot well tell whether the picture is like him. J. B. 1677.]

## LIX.

CAROLUS S. PANCRATII S. R. E. DIACONUS CARD. GUALTERIUS ARCHIEP. FIRMAN. URBEVETAN. II. MARTII, MDCLIIII.

Il Cardinalismo, p. 166.

He is of Orvietta,‡ and was, by the mediation of Donna Olympia, promoted to the cap, not that he was a person worthy of it or that the Pope had imployed him in any considerable affairs, but because it was his fortune to be allied to the house of Pamphilio. Innocent the X$^{th}$ was averse really in his own mind from introducing persons of so small virtue as this and Maldachino § into the Sacred College amongst so many eminent persons and so many great princes. But Donna Olympia, who was paramount and did what she pleased, cast such a mist before the eyes of that innocent Pope that he discerned not what he did himself by the promotion of those two persons,

---

\* " Beginning not with fatherly exhortations so much as with comminations and threatenings."

† " It is sufficient that there are no considerable faults to be found in him, unless it be that he is," &c.

‡ Orvieto.   § Art. lv. [J. B.]

uniting and fixing them upon her,* and, which is of greater importance, leaving so many worthy persons, till the error was committed, and all the streets of Rome in a commotion to have it rem[ed]ied. If the qualities of Maldichino and Gualtieri were compared, Gualtieri's, though they are good for little or nothing, are yet less ridiculous than the former. Donna Olympia imployed him in her [secret]† affairs, that is, she made him negotiate the selling of benefices; for, as bad as he was, he knew well enough to make his advantages of the elevation she gave him. From whom he learned also a great dexterity in shearing of his flock; and in his church of Firmo, of which he is Archbishop, he disdains not from time to time to receive presents from his clerks—not that he demands them, but, when they are offered, he never refuseth them. The Pope gave him that archbishoprick, not to recompence any desert that he found in him, nor that he thought him worthy to execute that pastoral charge, but only to send him packing from Rome—it going against the hour to see in the consistories and publique meetings such a creature sitting amongst so many Cardinals of renown. And he had done better yet had he by as honourable a banishment sent Maldechino as far from the Court. His chief goodness is that he knoweth his own weakness, and is ready therefore to take advice and to follow it.

[I so seldom saw him that I have forgot whether the picture is like him or not. J. B. 1677.]

## LX.

PETRUS TIT. S. SALVRIS IN LAURO S. R. E. PRE' CARD. OTTHOB. EP'S BRIXIEN' VENETUS. 19 FEB. 1652.

A noble Venetian, being Clerk of the Chamber, was promoted at the instance of the Commonwealth of Venice and his own, when

Il Cardinalismo, p. 160.

---

* "Ingroppandolo nella promotione di questi due personaggi, a lei sola attinenti." (Pt. ii. pp. 138-9.) These words relate not to the Pope, but to Olympia.

† Inserted from the English translation.

the Pope was desirous to satisfy all the Catholick crowns and potentates, amongst which, after France and Spain, Venice hath much the greater place, seeing God hath made them a bulwark to all Christendom. The nature of this Cardinal is, to carry himself with all possible complaisance to his own republick, in whatsoever he is imployed. He is not very rich, but indued with good qualities, and his parts are more than ordinary.* The Venetians have a great opinion of him, but the Court hath not, he having been confined, as it were, to his church at Brescia, without ever being imployed in any legation. His friends say that from that very thing, proceeding from the envy they have for him at the Court, the transcendant worth of his person may be known—which indeed is not unlikely; for princes trouble not themselves so much to find out persons of any excellent endowments, as to find such weak, poor-spirited persons as they can command at their pleasures,—from whence it happens that they which preside do suffer them to be discontented that are otherwise in favour.†

In the conclave of Alexander, he had a great share in uniting that party that thwarted and crossed the designs of the crowns, who were not at all satisfied either with him or his party. He, having formerly been *Auditor di Rota*, was afterwards made Datary,‡ wherein he may demonstrate his worth at court, he having already given some essays of his virtues.

[I have several times been at Brescia, both going into and coming out of Italy, it being on the confines of the Venetian state, next to the dukedom of Milan, and may be called a magazine, where is a perpetual appearance of war in the time of peace—every shop being

---

\* " E. a mio giudizio uno de' piu degni soggetti che habbia il Collegio, leggista, politico, manieroso, e per ogni conto stimabile, anzi che, se con Spada non peccasse d'haver troppo credito à se medesimo, sarebbe assai più lodato." (Estampes-Valençay, fol. 47 b.)

† " Di dove nasce, che quelli che presidono, lasciano scontenti anco quelli che ricevono gratie." (Pt. ii. p. 215.)

‡ The statement in the Cardinalismo is, that he was made Datary by Clement IX., in acknowledgment of his support at the Pope's election.

stored with arms of all sorts, their chiefest and greatest traffick being arms, and are esteemed the best in Europe.

I was at Rome in the conclave of Alexander the VII., where I often saw this Cardinal. The picture is like him. J. B. 1677.]

## LXI.

ANTONIUS TIT. S, AUGUSTINI S. R. E. PRESB. CARD. BICHIUS.
EPUS. AUXIMANUS SENENSIS. IX APRILIS, MDCLVII.

He is nephew to a sister of Alexander VII., and brother to Prior Bichi, a Knight of Malta, and one that has the commendation of a very worthy man. The Pope's design was to make a Cardinal of the Knight; but the whole family of the Chigi (that is, the Pope's) conspired against it. The principal cause of the opposition of the nephews to exclude the Knight proceeded from a suspicion they had that, if that cousin of theirs should arrive at a cardinalship (that is, into such an eminent degree as would authorise him to speak his mind freely), he would not fail to create some differences betwixt them; and that the rather, because they had already more jealousies of one another than the Pope or their consanguinity would allow,— the Knight having a strange dexterity at setting other people by the ears. Wherefore the nephews recommended his brother to his Holiness, who, to revive the memory of his sister, made him a Cardinal.

Whilst this man was Bishop of Osimo, he gave good demonstrations of his ability in governing the Church, having wrought himself into the hearts of the people, especially the clergy, who magnified him for one of the best bishops that ever was in that place. After he was promoted, his Holiness began to imploy him in several important and politick affairs. He receives all persons that come to him with great civility, and indeavours to ingratiate with the ministers of princes, without giving occasion of jealousy either to one or other. He seems a great enemy to tumult and noise, yet fails not upon occasion to speak his own sense, and that with some violence of words. He was very devout and pious when he was a bishop, and they are much increased since he was a Cardinal. In short, he also is driving at the popedom; but I fear he will miscarry, as all the rest have done that have taken his way.

[I cannot say whether the picture be like him. The last time of 4 of my being at Rome, being there 1660, when the King was restored, and I think I saw this man but twice. J. B. 1677.]

## LXII.

CAMMILLUS TIT. S. MARCELLI S. R. E. PR'BR. CARD. MELTIUS ARCHIEPS. CAPUAN. MEDIOLANENSIS. IX APR. MDCLVII.

[*No account given.*]

## LXIII.

SCIPIO TIT. S. SABINAE S. R. E. PRESBITER CARD. DE ILCIO ARCHIEPIS. PISARUM SENEN. IX APRILIS, MDCLVII.

Il Cardinalismo, p. 180.

From the beginning of his yeught,* he gave great tokens of his capacity to try his fortune in the habit of a prelate, and, by his own inclination as well as his parents setting him forward, he went to Rome, where by degrees he wrought himself into the most conspicuous and most intricate affairs there. He was sent nuncio to Venice, where he carried himself with so much satisfaction to the Senate that he was adored amongst them as an oracle. Yet his negotiation for the churches, for provision for the bishops, succeeded not so well, some remaining without pastors all the time of his nuntiature, for the Venetians are careful and vigilant not to suffer Rome to set his foot upon any privilege of theirs; in which

* See MS.

difference between the Pope and them, his prudent and wise transactions kept it from a rupture.

Pope Innocent the X[th], about the end of his pontificate, sent him nuntio into Germany, where he remained about two years, in which time Alexander the VII., his kinsman, being made Pope, he thought he could not discharge his conscience without promoting one of his worth with a cardinalship; yet he would not promote him for the title of *nuntio*, but as he was a grateful man, and worthy of that honour; and besides, he was desirous his kindred should have their share in that promotion. This is most certain, this Cardinal's qualities do render him worthy, not only of the purple, but of the Popedom; in the obtaining of which (if the election happen in his time,) he could meet with no impediment but his being of Siena, for, to speak truth, the Court hath been glutted with Popes from Siena.

He is charitable and kind, and a great lover of his friend. He is of great authority in the consistory, and his opinion in the congregations is more respected than any one's. His kindred trouble him not much, but perhaps would do more if he were Pope. He can dissemble well, and seemeth to take no notice of any injury, though it be written very deep in his heart.

[Though I was (the last time of 4), at Rome 1659 and 1660, at our King Charles the Second's restauration, yet I cannot say the picture is like; for I do not rem[em]ber that ever I saw him above once. J. B. 1677.]

## LXIV.

HIERONYMUS TIT. S. AGNETIS EXTRA MOENIA S. R. E. PRESB. CARD. FARNESIUS, ROMANUS. IX. APRILIS, MDLVIII.

In his youth he was wild and unconstant, but grew more prudent and discreet by degrees, indeavouring to acquire those virtues that are necessary at Rome to the gaining of a cap, which design breaks the

Il Cardinalismo, p. 180.

sleep of many a prelate. Innocent the X[th], who was so difficult to accommodate with another man's opinion, had so great an esteem at first for this person, that in all his affairs he would have his judgment still, and prized it so as to prefer it to his own,—" because " (said he,) " his counsels are delivered with prudence, integrity, and learning;" and some wits, that envied his good fortune, made libels on him, calling him most commonly the fifth evangelist. And some presaged a change, as it fell out; for Innocent, being disgusted by him, either because he would not do as he would have him, or that Donna Olympia had given him a lift so far, that he turned his love into disdain, reviling the person as extravagantly as ever he had commended him.

Alexander the VII[th], that pretended to understand the merits of a man as well as anybody, and was resolved to use no man's judgement but his own in the election of his Cardinals, was no sooner lept into the chair but he made him his *maggior domo;* and, because he knew he had a brain capable to dispatch severall imployments By that Pope's favour he facilitated the acquisition of the Terra Farnese, which was his own jurisdiction, and found out a way to exclude the Duke of Parma, who was to succeed him in case the right line failed. When the Pope gave him a cap, he sent him legate to Bologna, in which he carried himself to the satisfaction of his Holiness, and likewise of the people. He is a man of a very great brain, which would be a prejudice to him if the chair were vacant, because they all know too much wind does more hurt to a ship than too little. In all his negotiations he has behaved himself like a true ROMAN. He is old, and of a weak complexion. He is somewhat refractory in his opinions, and is angry with everybody when things go not as he adviseth, and sometimes he is angry alone.

[I saw him but once or twice, on the last of my 4 times being at Rome, in 1660, and, as I remember, the picture is like him. J. B. 1677.]

## LXV.

NICOLAUS TIT. S. EUSEBII S. R. E. PRESB. CARD. A BALNEO EP'US SENOGALLIEN. XIX APRIL. MDCLVII.

[*No account given.*]

## LXVI.

HIERONYMUS TIT. S. HIER. ILLIRICOR. S. R. E. PRE' CARD. BONVISIUS EP'S LUCAE. LUCEN. IX APRILIS, MDCLVII.

A nobleman of Lucca, repaired to Rome with design to try his fortune, as others of his countrymen were wont. He applied himself to the Barberini, then regnant. Cardinal Antonio [the then Pope's nephew], knowing him to be inclined to secrecy, had confidence in him, and intrusted him in matters of no ordinary importance, and particularly in the wars with the princes of Italy. He bought the clerkship of the chamber, in which he gained reputation, being very well practised in matters concerning the profession in law. Afterwards he discharged himself in several offices that he executed with good reputation; but in the time of Innocent the X[th] he could not indure that insatiable liberty that Donna Olympia used in getting of money with such diminution of the treasure of the Church,—and particularly, when he saw the bartering for the taxes upon provisions, he generously refused the prefecture, that he might not be instrumental in so infamous a business. Which Innocent, and Donna Olympia especially, taking in dudgeon, contrived to do him a displeasure, of which he having notice retired.*

But this renuntiation of the prefecture gave Bonvisi a great reputation at the Court, and [made] him to be looked upon as a man of great conscience and integrity; and, amongst all, Cardinal Chigi took a particular kindness for him, and, as soon as he was made

[Il Cardinalismo, p. 179.]

---

* "They began to contrive some way of doing him a displeasure; which he, having notice of, retired, and thereby escaped that rock he might otherwise have fallen upon."

Pope by the name of Alexander the Seventh, he recalled him into his service; upon which he revived those hopes he thought had been utterly extinct, and, being arrived at Rome, in the first promotion he was created Cardinal, to the great joy of the whole Court.

He hath all the good parts that are requisite to make a man esteemed, and of princes especially,—using all dexterity, and avoiding with all possible caution to show himself devoted to either of the crowns of France or Spain, desiring to live in a neutrality. But all the lustre of his good qualities is somewhat obscured in his loving too much his ease, and not caring so be troubled in business, so that he will scarce arrive at the papacy; and because his nephew is full of a thousand vices.

[I never saw him but once or twice, at the last of my 4 times being at Rome, an° 1660, and think the picture is like.]

## LXVII.

SFORTIA E SOCIETATE JESU TIT. S. SUSANNAE S. R. E. PRESB. CARD. PALLAVICINUS, ROMANUS.   IX. APRILIS, MDCLVII.

Il Nipotismo, p. i. l. iii. p. 133.

Padre Pallavicino, a Jesuit, was Pope Alexander's (VII.) confessor, before that he was made Cardinal for the writing of [two volumes in folio in Italian of] the History of the Council of Trent, which, indeed, may well be called his, for the greatest part of it is not history and relation, but an abundance of words by which he indeavoureth to prove that the history of Padre Paulo upon the same subject was and is false. But he stumbles at every step he goeth, and is so ill furnished with arguments, that, for my part, I must confess that I never believed Padre Paulo's History to be real, sincere, and true but since I read the Jesuit's. And he that will profit by them, let him read them both with an equal disinteressment.

But in the putting forth that book he had one ill accident, which was, that he had taken occasion to praise Pope Alexander in divers places, and extoll him to the skies as an angel rather than a man for denying his own blood and relations and keeping them at a distance. The sheets were printed, and the book was coming out, when the Pope went to receive his kindred at Castel Gandolfe, and brought them to Rome. This cast the Father into a strange perplexity, and the rather because the Pope had asked him his advice about the business, as being his confessor.* This confounded him, for if he counselled him to receive them, that must give his book the lye; if he exhorted to the contrary, that was the way to offend the Pope and his kindred, and so lose all his fortune. At last he resolved, by counselling the Pope to receive his kindred, and by printing again those sheets over which made mention of the Pope's alienation from all human affections. But the printer refused to do it at his expenses; so the Father was fain to be at the charges of reprinting of about twenty sheets.†

[I was told at Rome that his story (not history) of the Council of Trent got him the Cardinal's cap. He is a hard-favoured, lean man, tall, with a thin-haired flaxenish beard. The General of the Jesuits order and he, you may be sure, were great. The picture is like him. J. B. 1672.]

## LXVIII.

Franciscus Tit. S. Joannis ante Portam Latinam S. R. E. Pr'br. Card. Paulutius Forolivie'. Praef. S. Cong. Concilii. 9 Aprilis, 1657.

[*No account given.*]

---

\* Vide art. i. [J. B.]

† "So that the good Father was fain to have recourse to some of his devout children, who, out of charity, paid for the reprinting of," &c.

# CATALOGUE OF DR. BARGRAVE'S MUSEUM.

This little booke, with what is contained in it, my cabinet of medals, antiquities, rareties, and coynes, I give unto the Library of Christchurch, Canterbury, *after my death.*\* Apr. 29, 1676.

Dr.\* JOHN BARGRAVE, *Canon.*\*

\* The words in Italics were a later addition.

# RARA, ANTIQUA, ET NUMISMATA BARGRAVIANA,

Romae et aliis Italiae locis diversis, nempe 4 Itineribus, collecta, per me Johan. Bargravium, Generosum Cantianum, olim Coll. S$^{ti}$ Petri Cantabr. Socium, Bello civili, Anno 1643°, per Rebelles expulsum, restaurato vero Carolo 2° restauratum; S. T. P. et canonicum Eccles. Metroplit.* Cantuariensem,* 1662.

---

I being 4 journeys from London to Rome and Naples, I found that where labourers digged either within or without the city, or up and down the country, amongst the ruins of the old Roman temples, amphitheatres, theatres, aqueducts, cirques, naumacheas, baths, &c., to lay the foundations of any new churches, colleges, monasteries, nunneries, pallaces, or the like, amongst those ruins those labourers often found great and small statues or images,—some of marble, some of brass,—of the old heathen gods and goddesses, and of divers emperors and emperesses, and votes or vows presented to them. The Pope's, and every Cardinal's and Prince's pallaces are nobly adorned with them.

Those labourers likewise dig up, and the plowmen plow up, and those that work in the vineyards dig up, great numbers of ancient Greek and Roman medals, some bigger, some less, of gold, silver, and brass, of which there are great collections amongst the anti-

* *Sic.*

quarians at Rome, and many learned books written upon them in all languages, with the cuts of the coins, together with the rinverce, or other side of them, which are very historical. My often seeing of them put me likewise into a humour of curiosity, and making this collection insuing, which I have now, 1676, in a cabinet in my study at my canonical house, at the metropolitical church of Christ, Canterbury.

## *Brass Images, &c.*

(1). *Imprimis*, an infant Romulus, in brass, in a sitting posture, digd out of Quirinus his temple, on the Quirinal hill, when those ruins were removed to make way for the very fine, pretty, rich church or chapel of S<sup>ta</sup> Maria della Vittoria, built in memory of the great victory the Emperor had over the King of Bohemia near Prague, where are hanged up in triumph the banners, ensigns, and colours that were there taken, whereof I remember was, mitres, crosses, the Pope's triple crown, &c., all turned upside down, with this motto—*Extirpentur*.\* The little figure very ancient.

(2). *Item*, a very ancient Æsculapius, in brass—the medicinal god—in a long robe, with his baton or knotty staff in his hand, with a snake round about it, dugg out of the ruins of his temple in the island of the river of Tyber, where now standeth the hospital of St. Bartholomey.

(3). A very ancient brass image of Hercules, one foot broke off, with his club in his hand; esteemed for its good features, and very like other marble statues and brass medals that I have seen of Hercules, whereof there is one amongst my drawers. This was dugg out of his temple near the Tyber, at the foot of the Aventine Hill at Rome—still standing, almost all, and made a chappell.

(4). *Item*, a brass flat piece, with the figure of a man drawing an ox by the horns; very ancient, being dugg out of another temple of

---

\* This agrees with Raymond's description, p. 105.

Hercules that stood upon the Aventine Hill, on the place where he killed the thief Cacus, where now standeth a church dedicated to St. Stephen, which by its title beareth the memory of the old story of Cacus, it being still called S<sup>to</sup> Stefano nel Caco.

(5). *Item*, two old Roman sacrificing priests in their robes, and patina in hand: the one a very good one,—if not ancient, yet cast from ancient; the other modern.

(6). Hercules Juvenis, with his club and lion's skin; another of them; both supposed modern.

(7). *Item*, a maymed Mercury, with one arm and one legg; ancient, dugg out of his temple.

(8). An ancient brass Dolphin, dedicated to Venus, and dug out her temple. *Nam Venus orta mari.*

(9). An handsome ancient *busto* (as called at Rome) of Augustus —that is, the head and shoulders—in brass.

(10). *Item*, a Leda, with her swan; supposed to be modern, but cast from ancient.

(11). A flat brass piece, of several Cupidons scaring one another with a vizard; being a bachanalia piece, dugg out of the Temple of Bacchus.

(12). A little key, dug out of the Temple of the Moon.

(13). *Item*, a brass wreathed snake, in circles, having a head at both ends; dedicated to Eternity.

(14). *Item*, a flat piece of brass, with the rapture of Proserpine by a Centaure.

(15). The knuckles of the legg bone of mutton, which we call a *cockal*, with which children use to play; such an one dugg out of the ruins, in brass, that sheweth the Romans used them in games called *Ludi talarii*.

(16). The River of Tyber, carved on a piece of coral; ancient.

(17). Two Priapisms, in brass, being votes or offerings to that absurd heathen deity. . . . modern, from ancient.

(18). A Roman ægle, in brass; modern.

(19). A piece of a kind of jasper stone, almost like a heart, polished, being a piece of that famous obelisk that now standeth in the chiefest place of Rome, called Piazza Navona, *olim Circus Agonalis*, set up there on a most magnificent fabrick, like a rock, out of which floweth 4 fountains, very large, signifying by the figures of colossean statues of the 4 rivers of Europe, Asia, Africa, and America, by the hand of Cavalier Bernino, that famous architect, my neighbour and friendly acquaintance,—Pope Innocent the 10th being at that vast expense.

When I was at Rome, 1646, this obelisk lay broken in 4 or 5 pieces, with the fall of it, in the Circle of the Emperor Caralla,[*] near St. Sebastian and Metella's Tomb, now a noble antiquity, and called *Capo di Bove*. I took another stone, and with it broke off of the butt end of it this piece and as much more, and had this polished. The obelisk, as it lay then and as it is now, is full of Egyptian hyerogliflicks, of which Father Kercherius, that eminent Jesuit, and of my acquaintance, hath writt a large folio. All the other guglios,[†] or obelises, at Rome seem to be all of the same sort of stone, and are stupendious to imagine how they could possibly be hewn in that bigness and hight out of any rock, though it may be they might afterward be hewn into that pyramidical proportion and shape that they now bear. All full of Egyptian hyroglificks, that largest of all before St. Peter at the Vatican excepted, which is one intyre precious stone—at least, better than marble, and I think (by my piece) a jasper; and yet is esteemed to be higher by 3 or 4 foot than the maypole in the Strand at London. Another is dexterously placed on the Via Flaminia, at the Porto dell Populo, in a poynt to be seen from 3 of the great streets of Rome.

Another dispute is, how it was possible to transport so vastly weighty things from Egypt to Rome as one of those stones are, they having then no such ships as we have now, their byremes and tryremes being but pittiful boats, yet sufficient to make them

---

[*] *Sic.* It is now called the Circus of Maxentius, or of his son Romulus.
[†] The word is properly not guglio, but guglia.

masters of the seas in those times. There are several treatises on this subject; and the most probable that I find is, that they were brought upon warfts or rafts of many pines and firs, fastened by art together, and, the stones being laid upon them, they, with a stearer or 2 or 3 at the end of those rafts, came *terra, terra, terra* (as the Italians term it) along the coast, or, at least, from promontory to promontory, until they came to Ostia, and so 10 miles up the Tyber to Rome. Many long and large warfes or rafts of these fir and pine trees I have found troublesome to our boats on the Danube, the Rone or Rhodanus, on the Rhine, and Elve, down which rivers an infinite abundance of that tymber passeth daily thus fastened together, and on some of them they build 2 or 3 little hutts or cabans and dress their meat. Thus as to these pyramids' transport.

Another of these vast stones layeth all along full of hyerogliphics, in that which is now Prince Ludovicio's, formerly Sallust's garden.[*] And, to see how Rome layeth under its own ashes, one walketh in the streets over one of these famous Egyptian obelisks every day, in a little by passage of a narrow descent that is between Antonina's famous piller and the Rotunda. I could go directly to it if I were there, but I have forgotten the name of the place. There one day an antiquarian had me down a poor man's cellar, and there showed me 4 or five yards of one of these pyramids.[†] How far it runneth under ground they know not. It was full of hieroglyphics, and it pittied me to see how the stone was cut and mangled for the convenience to set wine vessels on it. The poor man getteth his rent by showing of it to strangers that are curious—as I confess I always was, and would wish every gentleman traveller to be so.

(20). *Item*, two large loadstones, one armed with steel, in a black velvet case, which I hanging in my study upon a piece of silk, in a perpendicular thread, when it standeth still, the north point hangeth still due north; by which I found that our cathedral of Christ Church, Canterbury, doth not stand due east and west, but the east

[*] This is now erected in front of the church of Sta. Trinita de' Monti.
[†] This now stands on the Monte Citorio.

end is at the least 2 poynts of the compass too much to the southward. Now, where it is generally received that the loadstone draweth iron to it, by this perpendicular posture of the stone upon a thread, and putting a key or any other piece of iron to it, the iron draweth the loadstone quite round, as far off as you please, so that it seemeth there is no compulsion on either side, but a mutual reciprocal compliance between them both, which we are fain to call sympathy. Now, on the other side, I have in my cabinet another triangular, unequilateral, bumped-up, large loadstone that weigheth almost half a pound, which is a rude thing to look on, but of good value. This is unarmed, but it is strange to see how great an antipathy there is between the north point of this stone and the other that hangeth perpendicular in the velvet bagg, this making that (at a great distance) fly from it with violence as often round as you please; and, on the other side, there is a great sympathy between the south point of the one stone and the north point of the other. For this seemeth strange to me, that every loadstone, be it in pieces bigger or less, have still their north and south point, according to the two poles axill of the world. With the hidden qualities of these 2 stones I used sometimes to make sport with young gentry in telling them their fortunes, &c. as if there had been an intelligence between them and me—" If so and so, then do so and so." And truly it is wonderful to me to think that it was the loadstone that found out America and the Straights of Megallan, and by virtue of which several nations, especiall[y] England, have almost found out the north-west passage of the West Indies, and so to go a much shorter cut from England by the West Indies to the East. And if the *Terra Incognita*, or the fifth part of the unknown world, be ever found out, it must be done by virtue of the loadstone.

(21). *Item*, a piece of a heavy mineral stone, that looketh like a loadstone, but hath no such attractive virtue; but at Hall, near Insprugg in Tiroll, among the hearts of the Alps, I had the curiosity to be droven in a wheelbarrow almost 2 miles under ground, to see the labourers there in the gold and silver mines belonging to the Archduke of that country. It was horrid to go thither, and more horrid to see, but they told us the Emperor and the Empress, and all the royal family of the house of Austria use out of curiosity to go thither. I and my companion having on canvass frocks to keep us from the wet and filth, we having a mountain of the Alps 3 or 4 mile high over our heads, and a torrent of water under us, and a bridge of boards most of the way. When we came into the vast high vaults, where hundreds and hundreds of men or Vulcans were at work, one of the overseers (a genteel person), out of courtesy, would have let us see their art by blowing up a part of the mine by gunpowder; but we durst not venture it. Another great mystery to me was, that I saw in the several high vaults, about the middle, a coggell of wood hanging in a small rope; and I asking wherefore those bastons or pieces of wood hung there, I wondered the more they told me, that, as the loadstone in the iron mines directed to the veins of iron, so these coggells of wood directed them to the veins of gold and silver; and they seemed to be loth to tell us what sort of wood it was, but at lenght we were told (whether truly or no I know not), that it was of a ground ash.

This stone is a piece of the one they digg out of those mines, out of which, by the force of fire, is extracted the silver and the gould, being separated from the dross, which is there cast up and down into great hills near the places where the fornices for melting are.

(22). Ten miles, almost, round about Rome, under the vineyards and cornfields, are hollow caves, streets, rooms, chappells, finely paynted, &c., which is called *Rome underground*, or the *Catacombe*, wherein to the poor Christians in the times of persecution fledd to hide themselves, to perform the Christian duties of preaching and prayer and sacraments. And some of these underground streets were for their burials,—not on the flat, as we bury on the ground, but the corps were at their lenght immuralld in *thecas*, or, as it were, in hollow shelves dug into the wall on both sides; and it is a horrid place to go to, and dangerous, for fear of damps, for which we had little bottles of essences and spirits to put to our noses, and tynder purses (as the mode is), with flint, steel, and match, to lighten our torches and candles when they went out. My curiosity held me there about 3 hours at one time in one of these cymeteries; I going down a pair of stayre, and so walked some streets in Rome underground, a second story deep, until we came to water, which made us return. But the best and freest from danger, and easiest to be seen, are those at St. Agnese, out of the Porta St. Agnese, where in half an hour I came to a street that I could tell 10 stories of corps high; and so all along, about 30 or 40 in lenght. I and other gentlemen with me observed that, though there were divers epitaphs and writings, with Pº, Xto, Pº, Nº, with a turtle dove and an olive branch in its beack, and a palm branch, with Po †º, yet, I taking all along on the one side, and my companions on the other, we could meett with never an *Orate pro anima*—praying for the souls of the dead not being then known, in the primitive times, there being no such thing as purgatory then known in the world,— that being of a later invention, to bring a vast revenue to the Pope or *Camera Apostolica*.

From this Rome underground I brought a very fair small ancient lamp, and a small bottle with a long neck—both of them of a very fine red earth; which, by Dr. Plott, I sent as a present to the cabinet of Oxford Library. One other earthen lamp, and a glass bottle with such a long neck, and a broken one in two pieces, I have in my cabinet. These bottles are called *lachrymatorij*, or *tear-bottles*, because the friends and relations of the defunct were in ancient time accustomed at the funeral to carry each of them a *lachrymatorio* in his hand, to save his tears that he shed for his deceased friend, and then leave those bottles behind them with the immuralld corps. David seemeth to have allusion to this ancient custom when he saith, Psalm 56, 8, " Thou hast put my tears into thy bottle."

(23). Another thin piece of jasper stone, unpollished, it being sawn off of that piece of the *guglio*, pyramid, or obelisc that standeth now in the Piazza Navona at Rome; of which I have spoken at large, page the 7 [118], &c., where you may be satisfied about those wonderful obelises.

(24). *Paste antiche Romane incognite*,—several pieces of a flat ancient Roman paste (as they term it) unknown,—*i. e.* that the art of it is lost or forgotten. These several pieces I pict up amongst the antiquarians. They are of all sorts of colours, as you may see where they are broken. They are on the outside rude and rough, but, being polished, it looks like a precious stone, as you may see by several small pieces of them that I caused to be polished, and cut in the figure of a heart. One green, with spots like stars; the other a plain blew. They seem to be a kind of glass, or rather of that material of which enamell is made; but whichsoever the matter is I know not. But they put an esteem upon them, and I [was] made pay dear for them.

(25). Small cinders and pummy stones of Mont Aetna, in Sicily, where I never was; but I had them from my Lord of Winchelsy, my noble friend, who hath bin there.

(26). Several pieces of cinders, pummystone, and ashes of the Mount Vesuvius, near Naples, which was 4 times the poynt of my reflection,—I facing about for England from the topp, or crater, or *reragine* (as they term it) of that mountain; of which I have spoken at large in my *Itinerario d'Italia.*\*

(27). Several rude pieces of mountain chrystall, as they grow sexanguler always among the Alps; amongst which there is one is a very clear, handsome, elegant piece, something longer than my middle finger, 4 or 5 inches compass, sexangular, inaequilateral, cylindrical, pyramidical.† This I met with amongst the Rhaetian

---

\* See the Introduction to this volume. Raymond says, "This mountain was the *ultimus metis* of our voyage to Naples." (P. 163.)

† The same article is described on a separate paper as "a cristall as it naturally groweth, sexangular, which I met with on the Penine Alps, on the Sempronian Mount, now called Mount Samplon." Sir Henry Wotton, among his bequests, mentions "a piece of crystall, sexangular (as they grow all), grasping divers things within it, which I bought among the Rhaetian Alps, in the very place where it grew." (Walton's Lives, 109, ed. Oxf. 1821.) For the passage of the Simplon, as it was in those days, see Raymond, p. 218.

Alps. One would wonder that nature should so counterfett art. There is no man but [that?] seeth it but would veryly believe that by tools and art it had binn put into that figure. I remember that the Montecolian man that sold it me told me that he ventured his life to clamber the rocks to gett it. Where it grew I cannot say; but where it was, it was covered, he said, with long sedgy grass growing about it, under the dripp of an higher rock, where the snow continually melteth and droppeth; and so all the mountayn chrystall is increased *ab extra* by an external addition, and groweth not from any rock.

(28). *Item*, a small gold Salerno ring, written on the outside, not like a posey in the inside, but on the out—*Bene scripsisti de* ME, *Thoma*. The story of it is, that Thomas Aquinas, being at Salerno, and in earnest in a church before a certain image there of the blessed Virgin Mary, his earnest devotion carried him so far as to ask her whether she liked all that he had writ of her, as being free from original sin, the Queen of Heaven, &c.; and intreated her to give him some token of her acceptance of his indeavours in the writing so much in her behalf. Upon which the image opened its lipps, and said, *Bene scripsisti de* ME, *Thoma*.

Salerno layeth a little beyond Naples, on the Mediterranean sea; and the goldsmiths of the place, for their profit, make thousands of these rings, and then have them touch that image which spake. And no marchant or stranger that cometh thither but buyeth of these rings for presents and tokens. An English marchant gave me this at Naples. The *Schola Salernitana* was anciently famous for physicians.

(29). *Item*, a gold ring, with the cutt of an ancient Graecian head on a garnet stone sett in it. An° 1650, being the year of jubilee, I had the honour to conduct the Earl of Chesterfield, Phillip Lord Stanhop, into Italy; and at Rome he presented me with this stone, telling me that it was sold him not only for a Graecian head, but for Aristotle's. I sett it in gold at Rome, as the jeweller advised me, in that transparent posture as it now hath, that so, the stone being pellucid, the head is much the plainer to be seen both ways. The side next to the finger will soil, and must sometimes be cleaned. The cutt is certainly a very very ancient *intaglia* (as they use to call such cutts at Rome), melting away the *g* in the pronunciation, and pronouncing it almost with a *ll—intallia*.

(30). *It., Confetti di Tivoli*, a box full of sugar plums of the town of old Tybur, now called Tivoli. They seem to be so like sugar plums that they will deceive any man that only seeth them, especially when the counterfeit amand and muske comfeits, made out of the same materials, are mixed amongst them. But the things themselves are nothing but the gravel or sand of the river Teverone, that runneth by Tyvoly (10 miles from Rome), and entreth into the river of Tybur. The plumms are of a chauchy or brimstony matter.

(31). Some of the floore of brimstone from that horrid sulfurious mountain at the other side of Naples called Sulfaterra, near Puteoly, now called Puzzuolo.

(32.) A bow ring of Persia, cutt out of an agate stone, which must be worn on the right thumb, with poynt upward. With this they draw at ease the strongest bow, and then, letting the bent thumb go, the arrow hath the greater violence.

(33). *Item, Atites, Lapis Aquilaris*, or the eagle stone, which I bought of an Armenian at Rome. They differ sometimes in colour. This is a kind of a rough, dark, sandy colour, and about the bigness of [a] good wallnut. It is rare, and of good value, because of its excellent qualities and use, which is, by applying it to childbearing women, and to keep them from miscarriages.* . . . . It is so useful that my wife can seldom keep it at home, and therefore she hath sewed the strings to the knitt purse in which the stone is, for the convenience of the tying of it to the patient on occasion; and hath a box she hath, to put the purse and stone in. It were fitt that either the dean's or vice-dean's wife (if they be marryed men)

* Some directions for the use of the stone are here omitted.

should have this stone in their custody for the public good as to neighbourhood; but still, that they have a great care into whose hand it be committed, and that the midwives have a care of it, so that it still be the Cathedral Church's stone.

(34). A very artificial anatomy of a human eye, with all its films or tunicles, by way of turnery in ivory and horn; together with the optick nerve which runneth into the brain, from which nerve the eye receiveth all its several motions. This excellent piece of art hath, when it is opened, fourteen pieces in it; but are, indeed, but a little more parcels in themselves than half so many. When you take them in sunder, the best way to keep them in order is to lay them all in a row, and then you shall find that the first piece and the last are in nature but one tunicle, and by art two, if you join them together; each half (but one) hath its correspondent—the *corneus* with the *corneus*, the two black ones likewise the same, and so the rest. The little apple of it also is included in two half tunicles. The usual way of anatomizing an eye, longways, by turning the films flat over one another, could not be so visibly imitated by art; but this, or roundway, was the invention of the College of Physicians at Padoüa, where an artist of High Germany imployed his skill in turning according to these doctors' orders, and at length produced this excellent piece of art—this anatomy of the human eye.

I have one also of an oxes eye, but that is very rude, gross, and not exact.

I bought this eye at Venice of a High Dutch turner, and, for the proof of it, I went a double share in two anatomies, of a man's body and a woman's, chiefly for this eye's sake, and it was found to be exact.

(35). *Item*, a fair large toadstool or mushroom of stone, very weighty, which is not a mushroom petrified, but grew always a stone, in this shape and figure. I bought it of an Armenian at Venice, who had many more of them to sell, of several sorts of colours and bigness, and divers other stones of pretty forms and figures.

(36). *Stylus Romanus*. The antiquarian that sold it me avowed it to be truly ancient; but thousands may daily be made, this being but a piece of steel about the lenght of one's middle finger, like a bodkin, with a blunt point at one end and a flat on the other end, the edge rabated on both sides, so that with the one end one may make an impression upon paper or the bark of trees, and with the other end one may easily rub out or make smooth what had been written. So that *vertere stylum* was as much as to recant of such and such things as he had formerly written.

(37). *Item*, a large piece of sea-horse tooth, said to be good against poison, next to an unicorn's horn.

(38). *Lusus Naturae*, a kind of a periwinkle's shell,* and divers other fashion stone shells, which I had out of the curiosities of art and nature at Douay † (not that in Flanders), 3 or 4 leagues off from Saulmur, or the river Loyre, in France, where there is an ancient amphitheater.

(39). A pretty little padlock and key of guilt mettle, and a piece of coral, given me by a nunn,—whose guifts are commonly costly, for you must return the double.

(40). *Item*, a pretty kind of nun's work purse, made of greenish silk, and a carved work mother of pearls shell, presented me likewise by a nun, for which I paid for double, according to custom.

(41). *Item*, a pair of common Italian cards, which have, instead of our 4 sorts, 4 other names—(1) *Denari*, (2) *Coppe*, (3) *Spade*, (4) *Bastoni*—money, cups, fauchions or swords, and clubbs (or rather cogils); and, having the same number with ours, one may play all the English games with them, as well as the Italian.

(42). *Item*, Monsieur Demarests' ‡ learned and ingenious pack of cards, called *Jeu d' Armoire de l'Europe*, composed, as I was told in

---

\* This was, of course, a fossil shell.

† The name of this place ought to be written *Doué*.

‡ Jean Desmarets, for whom see Bayle, x, 256, seqq. ed. Paris, 1820; or Nouv. Biographie Générale.

France, upon this occasion. Cardinal Mazarine being in place of a guardian to the now reigning King of France, in his minority, (Louis XIV$^{th}$,) and the king being grown up to the age of years in which he took delight to play at cards, he, that the king, at his playing of cards, might also learn something else of worth and knowledge in his very play, put this virtuoso, Mons$^r$ Desmarests, to invent a pair of cards that might have that effect; upon which he invented these cards, which, having the ordinary marks of hearts, clubs, spades, and diamonds, he maketh hearts to be France, and the king to be king of hearts; clubs to be Italy, and all its principalities; spades to be the northern parts,—Germany, England, Denmark, Sweden, &c.; and diamonds to be Spain, Portugall, and all their territories. This done, when the king went to play at cards, a fair mapp of Europe was to be laid upon the carpet, and, when the cards were dealt unto the king, he was not to play his game at cards until he was first instructed in blazonry, geography, and history of this or that card he had in his hand,—blazoning the arms as it is upon each card; then, to find out the place in the mapp of Europe that the card signified; and, lastly, to tell some little history of that place; and then, to play the ordinary game. So that the king learned armory, geography, and history, all at playing of cards, there being a little book of Mr. Desmarests, which belong to this pack of cards, to teach his majesty how to use them. It is in French, with my cards.

What foundation this knowledge of the king's may have bin [*] layde as to his present wars, I know not; but now, *l' espé à la maine* (his sword in his hand), Lorraine is the 3 of hearts, the 17 provinces of the Low Countries is the 3 of spades, the Elect Palatine is the 6 of spades, the canton of the Swizzer is the 2 of spades, Catalonia is the 4 of diamonds, &c., and the terrible game of war goeth on. It had binn happier for Europe that he had never learned this *Jeu d' Armoires* than that it should have bin the

---

[*] This word seems superfluous.

occasion of his shedding so much blood. However, the king of spades, the Emperor and his northern allies, maintain the game against the king of hearts; and what card will be trump we know not at the end.

(43). *Item*, the skin, head, and legs of a camelcon, perfumed and stuffed. The creature was given me alive in Africa, and it liveth (not by the air, as the report goeth, but) by flies chiefly, as the Moores taught me how to feed it in this manner, by laying in the cage, or sometimes out of the cage in which I kept it, upon a paper some sugar and sweetmeats, which allureth the flies to come to it. The creature hath in its gorge or *gola* a toung that lieth 4 dobled, with a small fibulus button at the end of it, which hath on it a viscous matter. So soon as it seeth the flies at the sweetmeats it darteth forth that toung at a great distance, and with the viscous matter pulleth in the fly to her mouth, and cateth it; and so it will do many, one after the other, so that while we sailed homewards all along the Africa shore, and came out of the Mediterranean Sea by the Streights of Gibralter into the Atlantick Ocean, and then turning northward by Spain and Portugall—all that time (I say) that we were in those hot and southerly climates, although it was in January 1662, there were store of flies, and the creature fed on them heartily, and lived well. But as we sailed homeward into the more cold and northern climates, as the flies failed us, so that decayed, and at lenght for want of flies it died; and I had the chirurgeon of the shipp embalm it, and put the skin as you see it.

It seemeth to be a kind of lizard, but is as slow in pace as a tortes, winding its tail about the sticks of the cage, to help and secure its gradations. The ribs and the back are boned and scaled like fish. Although the story of its living by the air be fabulous, yet the other story of its changing itself into all colours is very true, as I have seen this of all manner of colours, like silk, and sometimes changeable colours, as the sun happened to shine upon it; and sometimes I have seen it coal-black. But the story is false that it hath a pellucid body, like cristal, and so it will be the colour of scarlet or any other cloth that you lay it upon. No, no such thing; but one way to make it change its colours was to anger it, and put it into a passion, by touching of it with a stick or a bodkin, or the like. Then it would fetch great breaths, many one after another, by which it made itself swell very much, and in its swellings out came the colours of all sorts, which changed as it was more or less provoked to anger. And when the passion was over, it would look as pale as a clout. It hath no eyelids, and therefore never winketh; but when it sleepeth, the ball of the eye being as round as round can be, it turneth that ball quite round, the inside outward, and so sleepeth. Matthiolus on Dioscorides sayth that it layeth eggs as a tortes doth, and is bred of those eggs.

(44). *Item*, the finger of a Frenchman, which I brought from Tholouse, the capital of Languedoc, in France. The occasion this: there is, amongst others, a great monastery of Franciscans, with a very fair large church and cloisters, the earth of which place is different from all others in this, that all the dead men and women's corps that are buried there turn not into putryfaction and corruption, and so into earth, as in all other places; but, on the contrary, the bodies that are buried there in the space of 2 years are found in the posture that they were laid into the grave, dried into a kind of momy, being all entire and whole, dried to almost skin and bone,— the nerves or sinews and tendons stiffly holding all the body together, that you may take it and place it standing upright against a wall. And in the vaults whither these dried corps are removed there are abundance of them, like so many fagotts, and as stiff and strong. Among which they shewed us the corps of a souldier, that died by the wound of a stabb with a dagger in his breast, upon the orifice of which one of his hands lay flatt, and when they pulled away the hand, the wound was plainly seen; but let the hand go, and it returned to its place with force, as if it had a resort or spring to force it to its proper place. I pulled the hand away several times, and the nerves and tendons were so strong that the hand returned with a lusty clap upon the wound. There likewise they shewed us the corps of a physician (of their acquaintance), which, when they put a clean piece of paper into one hand and a pen into the other, when he stood in such a posture as if he had seriously been a-writing a dose or prescription. The monks told us that in one vault the principals of their order stood all in a row, in the habit of the order, according to their seniority. They proffered me the whole body of a little child, which I should out of curiosity have accepted of, if I had then been homeward bound; but I was then outward bound for the grand tour of France (or *circle*, as they call it), and so again into Italy.

(45, 46). *Item*, two cylinders, with their wooden boxes,—the one of steel, which is most usual in England; the other of foyled isinglass, which I met with often in High Germany, from whence I brought this. The isinglass having a foyle of quicksilver and pewter put behind it, like a lookingglass, will afterward easily bend to the cylindrical piece of wood that you would fasten it to, and rendereth an excellent lustre, better than the steel. There are several uses of them in opticks. I used them with some several pictures, which are artificially painted like the greatest confusion of irregular lines and lineaments that may be. But, a cylinder being placed upon the square fitted for its pedestal, all the reflections of that seemingly confused work meet in the cylinder, and make a well-shaped, very handsome picture, in its due points and proportions. As to one of these cylinders belongeth, from the confusion on the plain, in the cylinder, an emperor on horseback on a white horse (which I brought from Rome, but they may be had in England).

The other, that I out of curiosity used to imploy, was in a very pretty experiment that I learned at Nurimberg and Augsberg, in High Germany, in making, by reflection of the sun's beam, as fair a rainbow as ever was seen in the sky, to be seen in a dark room— the darker the better—which I have done hundreth of times before many of quality, who have taken delight to see it. It is best done where there are close wooden shuts to the windows. It is done thus: the room being made very dark, there must be left only an auger hole, where the sunbeam may come clearly in through the shut,—the kesment being taken away, or a pannel of glass broken for the purpose, that the sun may be clear. Then lay to that hole a common prism or triangular artificial crystal, that casteth all kind of colours; the sun, without it, casteth through the hole a round spot of light, either upon the next wall, or on the floor; then that triangular crystal, being put to the hole, turneth that sunbeam into a round spot of divers glorious colours; then put a couple of small nails for the prism to rest upon, and keep that glorious spot; which done, take a cylinder, and hold it about a foot distance from the coloured spot, full in the sunbeam, or at what distance you find most convenient, and that will cast the reflections of that spot all round about the dark room, on the seeling and walls, in as perfectly various colours as ever you saw the rainbow. Upon which there happened a pretty passage to me once, which happened at Utrecht, which was this : there lived one Myn Here Johnson,[*] an extraordinary eminent painter, of my former acquaintance in England. I showed him this artificial rainbow ; he asked me how long I could keep it; I told him that I could keep it 2 or 3 hours : "Then," saith he, "I will send for my pallat of coulors, and draw it, for I have binn after endeavouring to draw one in the fields, but it vanished before I could finish it." Upon which I laughed. He asked me why I laughed ; I told him that he should see anon why I laughed, but assured him that I could keep the rainbow 2 or 3 hours; upon which he sent a servant for his pallat of coulors, and, being come, he tempered them to his purpose in the light. Then I darkened the room, but he could not see to paint, at which I laughed again, and I told him his error, which was, that he could not see to paint in the dark, and that I could not keep the rainbow in the light, at which he laughed also heartily, and he missed his design.

---

[*] Cornelius Jansen " in 1635 and the next following years resided with Sir Arnold Braems, a Flemish merchant at Bridge [Place], near Canterbury." (Dallaway's note in Walpole's Anecdotes of Painting in England, ii, 10, Lond. 1828.) His portrait of Dean Bargrave is in the Deanery at Canterbury, and was lent for the National Portrait Exhibition of 1866.

*Item*, a picture in a frame, of confused work; but a cylinder being placed on the square for its pedestal, there you shall see an emperor on horseback, and, if you moove your head up and down, the horse will seem to trott.

(48). An optick instrument of wood, turned round, and hollow within, and blacked, which serveth instead of a dark room; the small optick glass at the little end casting the shadows or figures and coulors of all outward objects upon a piece of clean paper fastened in with a hoop at the great end, with a covering over it, having a round hole in the middle, through which you may see all the reflections of the outward object as plain as may be; so that one may design them or paint them on the paper as they are represented, reversed, or their heels upward, and then, taking the paper off, it may be turned to the object's right posture, and not upside down. But the sun must shine clear upon the outward objects when they are to be fully and well represented, otherwise they are but dull. If the paper be very clean, and oyled over with good oyle, the species and colours are more perfect. The objects that are in motion, and those various, look the prettiest on the paper. As I happened to see it set against a large market place at Vienna, in Austria (the Emperor's court), where I bought it, the busy people in the market, and all their several coloured clothes, both of men and women, made me stand still and wonder what it meant. I went by the shop several times on purpose to see it, and at last I went into the shop and bought it, the owner showing me the use of it. With this instrument you may see the jackdaws fly about Bell Harry steeple,* when the sun shines, in any room of your house that hath a window that way.

(49). *Item*, a larger circular optick glass, about 4 inches diameter, made almost for the same purpose with the former, to receive outward specieses into a dark room; only this glass representeth them 4 times as bigg as the other, and at a much farther distance, which

---

*... the central tower of Canterbury Cathedral.

must be always observed as to the reception [of] the specieses. As this glass in a dark room, being placed to the hole, will render the reflexed species of the outward object full and large at a good distance, on a sheet of paper, or a fine napkin, or a large tablecloth, all the houses, windows, chimnies, trees, steeples, &c. that the sun shineth upon, and may be seen through the oager,[*] all will be fairly represented on that paper or tablecloth or napkin.

I bought this glass of Myn Here Westleius, an eminent man for optics at Nurenburg, and it cost me 3 pistolls, which is about 50$^s$ English. The gentleman spoke bitterly to me against Father Kercherius, a Jesuit at Rome (of my acquaintance), saying that it had cost him above a thousand pounds to put his optic speculations in practice, but he found his principles false, and shewed me a great basket of glasses of his failings. He shewed me wonderful strange glasses, some oval, some round, some square, some convex, some concave, which produced strange deceptions of the sight, unspeakable. As I well remember, when I put forth my hand to one glass, there came an arm and a hand out of the glass, as long as mine; and when our hands met, I seemingly could put finger to finger, palm to palm; and when I went to clasp hands together, I grasped nothing but air. Then, drawing my sword, and at a farther distance thrusting the point towards the glass, out from the glass came a sword and an arm, as to my sight, into the room; and we met, point to point, two or 3 paces from the wall, into the chamber—which was strange to me; and at lenght he made my whole person seemingly to come out of the glass into the room to meet me.

Another large glass he had, which, being hanged at one side of the room, and a fair perspective picture of the inside of a church, with its arches and pillars, hanged at the other, at a due distance, the species do so strangely come out from the glass that you seem to be walking in a church. Remove that picture, and place in its room a fair garden, with oranges and lemon trees, and fountains and walks,

[*] *i. e.* auger.

&c., and by the reflex of that glass, in the middest of the room, one seemeth to walk in a garden, and so in a grove, &c. For these glasses he asked me, for one 200, for the other 150, pistolls; and I think I should have given him his money, if my quality and purse had had a proportion suitable for such a purchase.

(50). *Item*, another optick glass, sowed into a piece of paceboard, to hang at a hole in a dark room, to the same purpose as the former.

(51). Westleius, of Neurenburg in High Germany, his optick wooden eye, which is only to set in the light into a darkened room, for the same use as formerly, only, as the sun removeth, so the wooden eye may be turned about to the sun, to keep the beams the longer on the optick glass.

(52). *Item*, a rare antiquity and curiosity: two Chinese books, in quarto, printed in the Chyna language upon I know not what material,—I think either silk, or rather on the barks of trees,*—every leaf being double, and having in every page an ill-favoured design or draught of picture. They were left me as a legacy and curiosity by one that had formerly binn my fellow traveller.

(53). *Item*, some shells of the strange diciille musell, bred in the heart of a stone. Thus one, or rather several, times at Rochell I walked out to the sea-side near the Digo, where I met with fellows who with beetles and axes and wedges were by the sea-side, as the tide went off, a cleaving of great stones. I asked them what they were doing and what they meant to cleave those stones. Their answer was, that they worked for their living, and that they were searching for diciiles, that is, for a sort of muscel shell-fish in those stones. I stood by, and saw then that, as the stone cleft, they found 1, 2, 3, or 4, some bigger some lesser. I asked them whether that they were good to eat. With that they ate them raw, as one doth an oyster, and I found them good meat, and afterwards sent them to our lodgings; and I saw them several times in the market to be sold, being very good well-relished fish. The stones from which

* It is the ordinary Chinese paper.

they are taken are full of holes, according to their proportion, some bigg some lesser.

(54). *Item*, an Indian tobacco pipe of leather to wind about one's arm, with a wooden pipe at the end of it, to be cleaned by washing it.

(55). Several pairs of horns of the wild mountain goats which the High Dutch call *gemps*, the Italians *camuchi*, the French *shammois*, from whence we have that leather. I had them amongst the Alps, the people telling me strange stories of the creature, what strange leaps they would take amongst the crags of the rocks, and how, to break a fall, they will hang by the horns, and, when they have taken breath, they unhook themselves and take another leap at a venture, and sometimes they will have great falls without any hurt, they still lighting upon their horns. Some of these horns are polished, and serve for several uses.

(56). A prohibited Venetian dark lanthorn, with a concave piece of steel at the back of the inside, which must be always kept very bright, and a convex half-globe of a crystaline glass on the outside; then a piece of wax candle being put in between them, the reverberation of the light from the steel through the crystal sendeth forth such a radiant light in a dark night that you may read anything at a great distance. It hath bin a murthering instrument with a pocket pistol and a poisoned stiletto—the revengeful party meeting and watching his adversary in the streets, on a sudden casteth such a dazeling brightness in his eye that he is astonished, whilst the other useth his instruments to kill him.

(57). *Item*, a Venetian stiletto poisoned without poison; that is, it is as bad as poisoned by reason that these oval little holes worked on the body of the steel of the stiletto maketh it give an uncurable wound, by reason that a point or tent, with its oils, balsalms, or otherwise curing salves, cannot reach the inward scars and inequalities of the dagger's hollow figures, and so it is impossible to cure such a wound.

(58). *Item*, a cravat, a shass or girdle, and a small pair of gaiters of curious work, by the inhabitants of the north-west (whether passage or no passage) of America, in the West Indies, made of porcupine quills very artificiously. In Italy there are butchers' shops particularly for venison, in which shops are every week hanged up store of these porcupines; but we foreigners did not much approve of the meat. The cravat, &c., with divers other things, were sent me by one Mr. Tymothy Conley, now a marchant in London, by way of gratuity, he being one of the 162 slaves that I redeemed from Argeers, when I went thither by King Charles 2 commission and 10,000$^{lb}$ of hierarchical money, 1662, for that purpose. Amongst the chains of the redeemed I kept only this man's, which I have now by me, and intend to have it hanged up over my grave *in memorandum*.

(59). *Item*, a pair of red leather pleyted buskins and 2 pairs of sleepers, with iron on the soles, such as the great ones—the Bashaes, the Agaàs, the Yabashawes, and Bulgabashaes—wear at Argeers.

(60). The picture in little of Shaban Agaà il Grand d' Algeers, or the King of Argeers, to whom I delivered his Ma$^{ties}$ (Charles II.) credential letter, and with whom I had chiefly to do in points of difficulty, though I bought slave by slave from each particular Turkish patron, as one buyeth horses in Smithfield. A poor painter, an Italian slave, stood privately to draw me this picture at several times when I had audience of Shaban Agaà. It is ill work, but the clothes and mode is like him, as he (and as all the country doeth,) sat cross legged on a Turkey carpet on a bench, I sitting at the turning of the bench by him, with my hat on, in my clerical habit; I finding him mostly very courteous. But in a 500$^{lb}$ business, that he would have had me pay for slaves that had made their escape, we were both very hot, and had like to have broken the peace, but at lenght my reasons prevailed. But at the end of all, when all the slaves were redeemed and sent on board his Ma$^{ties}$ man-of-war that attended us, it was a thousand to one but that the peace between us had binn broken, and I and my fellow commissioner, Dr. Selleck, had bin made slaves. It was but a greine in a pair of golden scales, whether aye or no—they having that night brought in an Englishman as a prize; but by God's blessing, and much difficulty, I played my part so well with threatening, that we got off. But poor consul Browne paid for it; for we were no sooner gone from their coasts but they broke the peace, and took all the English as formerly.

This Mr. Browne, the consul, went over in the same man-of-war with us, and we dieted and lay at his house. He had formerly lived long among them, and had their *Lingua Franca* perfectly. However, we were no sooner gone but they seized on all he had, shaved his head, and made him a slave, where he helped to draw timber and stones to a fortification, receiving so many blows a day with a bull's nerve, until he was beaten to death, and his body cast out upon a dunghill; which doubtless had binn our fortune if God had not binn pleased to bless us for the good work that we had done.

All the difficulties lay upon me, by reason that my brother commissioner had never binn beyond the seas, nor could speak a word of their language, and so understood not his danger until it was over.*

(61). *Item*, a fair book in folio, with the effigies of Alexander the 7th, and all the College of Cardinals at that time—A'n° D^{ni} 1658—to my knowledge very well cut, and exceeding like. I had occasion

---

* On the back of the drawing (which is on parchment), is the following inscription:
"Shaban Aga il Grand d' Algeers.

The King of Argeers, to whom I delivered his Ma^{ties} letters credential, when in 1662 I went his Ma^{ties} commissioner for the redemption of the English captives there with hierarchical and cathedral money, with which I redeemed and brought home with me all, viz. 162 slaves.

JOHN BARGRAVE, Gent., of Kent.
Canon of Christ Church, Canterbury.

An Italian slave, a painter, drew me this rude piece at Argeers, very like as to face and habit. The copies of which in large I gave, one to his Ma^{tie} Charles the Second, who hanged it in his private closet; another I gave to my patron, Archbishop Juxon; a third to Archbishop Sheldon; and a fourth I kept for myself, in memorandum of that Christian and noble imploy, 1662."

to have audience with several of them, and have writ what authors say of them in my hand.

(62). *Item*, a large folio in Italian, of medals, by Don Antonio Agostini, arcivescovo di Tarracona,—full of cuts of medals, with the reverse, writt by way of dialogue, *In Roma*.

(63). *Item*, a small turned instrument of wood, of about a handful, with a turned furrow in it for a cord that will bear a man's weight; it being useful in time of war for a prisoner to make his escape, by sliding down by a wall of any hight on a cord that shall not gall the hands, but the person may slide faster or softlier as he pleaseth, by griping or loosening this instrument. It was given me at Augsburg by a High-Dutch captain.

(64). *Item*, a manuscript in Italian, in folio, being the conclaves or intrigues of the elections of 13 Popes, beginning at Giulius the 3d, and ending with Paulus Quintus; bound up only *alla rustico*, as the Italians call it, in pastboard. At the end, *Di Roma, ii.x Maggio, MDCV*.

Five of them are translated into English, in loose sheets of paper.

(65). *Item*, a little manuscript in 5 sheets, unbound,* *Supplimenti d' alcuni Cardinali, che sono omessi nella* STATERA *in Stampa*.

(66). *Item*, a little manuscript in 6 sheets, unbound, *Instruttione del Sigr Balij di Valence, Ambr del Re Christianissimo, al suo Successore*.

(67). To hang upon my cabinet. My own picture upon copper, in little and *in seculo*, between my nephew and my neighbour, drawn at Siena, 1647, by the hand of Sigr. Mattio Bolognini, as written on the back side.

(68). To hang upon my cabinet. My own picture upon copper, in little and *in seculo*, drawn at Rome by a servant of my good friend Sigr. Giovanni Battista Caninij, an° 1650, the year of Jubely, as it is written on the back side.

[Then follows a list of "Numismata Bargraviana."]

* Nos. 65 and 66 are now bound together. See the Introduction.

[The following items are on detached papers:]

(69). [Ribbons with the inscriptions *Altezza della B. Vergine—Altezza del Bambino, &c.*] From Madonna di Loretto, for curiosity—to know the folly.

(70). For curiosity, because sold in the shops at Rome, so that for 2s. 6d. I had these 34 (pretended) reliques of saints' bones.

(71.) The native Virginian money, gold, silver, pearls, brought over by Mr. Alexander Coocke, that, being thrust out of his living at Dunkester, in Yorkshire, by the rebels,[*] went over chaplain to Sʳ Tho. Lonsford, and at the King's Restauration was made minister of Chislet, near Canterbury, in Kent, by Archbishop Juxon.

The black, that is the gold, the name forgot.

The long white, their silver, called *Ranoke*.

The small white, their pearl, called *Wopenpeake*.

The wife and daughter of Mr. Cooke gave me them as a present at a new year's time.

JOHN BARGRAVE, Præb. Cant., 1673.

[*] See the Introduction, p. xxviii.

# INDEX.

Acquaviva, Cardinal, 87, 88
Æsculapius, 116
Actites, 125
Agnes, St., Catacombs of, 122
Agostini, on Medals, 139
Albergati (Cardinal Ludovisi), 92
Albizi, Cardinal, 85-87
Aldobrandini, Cardinal, 84
Alexander VII., Pope, xi., xxv., 7, 8, 33, 68, 69, 96, 108, 110, 111, &c.
——— VIII., see Ottobuoni
Algiers, xiv.-xvii., 137, 138
Altieri, Cardinal (Clement X.), 10
——— family, 44
Ambrose, St., 82, 83
Aristotle, 121
Ash, used to discover precious metals, 121
Astalli, Cardinal, 65, 67, 68
Augustine, St., Baptism of, 83
Augustus, 117
Augustinian friars, 36
Avignon, residence of Popes at, 50
Azzolini, Cardinal, 67

Bagno, Cardinal di, 109
Barlane, 43
Barberino, Anna, 33
——— Antonio (senior) Cardinal, 27
——— Antonio (junior) Cardinal, 21, 26, 28-32, 35, 36, 47, 48, 50, 62, 73, 109, &c.
——— Carlo, Cardinal, 90, 91

Barberino, Francesco, Cardinal, 14-16, 17, 20, 26, 28, 41, 100, &c.
——— Maffeo, Cardinal (afterwards Urban VIII.), 41, 48, &c.; see Urban VIII.
——— Maffeo, Prince, 100
——— Taddeo, 48, 74, 94
——— family, 14, 44, &c.; pasquil on, 16; their influence in the conclave, 20; enmity with the Colonnas, 34
——— Palace, 73
Barcarola, Nina, 46
Bargrave, Frances, wife of the author, xvii.; her will, xx.
——— Isaac, Dean of Canterbury, x., xiv., xvii.-xix.
——— nephew of the author, xx.
——— John, of Bifrons, ix., x.
——— the author, ix.-xvii.; his four visits to Italy, x., xi., 6, &c.; his other travels, xi., xii.; returns to England, xii.; preferments, &c., xiii., xiv.; expedition to Algiers, xiv.-xvii., 137, 138; later years and death, xvii.; his will, xvii.-xix.; portraits of him, xi., 139; monument of Dean Bargrave erected by him, xx.; his Museum, xxi.; supposed share in Raymond's "Itinerary," xx., xxi.; his

account of the Pope and Cardinals, xxii.-xxviii.
Bargrave, Robert, son of the Dean, x.
——— nephew of the author, xix., xx.
——— Thomas, xviii.
Bernini, sculptor, 118
Bichi, Cardinal, 105, 106
Bisaccioni, xxv.
Bishops *in partibus infidelium*, 34
Bolognini, artist, 139
Books, prohibition of, 57, 58
Bordon, Mons. de, 46
Borromeo, St. Carlo, 82, 83
——— Cardinal, 82, 83
Bow-ring, Persian, 125
Brancacci, Cardinal, 38, 39
Brescia, 104, 105
Brisighella, 21
Bronze ["bell-metal"], 16
Browne, Consul at Algiers, 138
Buffuna, Cecca, 35
Buoncompagno, Cardinal, 42
Buonvisi, Cardinal, 109, 110

Caffarelli, Cardinal, 85
Cambridge, University of, x., xii.; Bargrave's legacy to St. Peter's College, xviii.
Capponi, Cardinal, 11-13, 16
Cardinal, meaning of the word, 2; account of the dignity, 2, 3; dress of the Cardinals, 3, 4; titles, 15; nations have certain Cardinals for their protectors, 16; Cardinal-deacons, 62
"Cardinalismo," xxiv., xxvii.

# 142 INDEX.

Cardinals, books on, xxiii.-xxvi.
Cards, Italian, 127; political, ib.
Carnival, 35
Carpegna, Cardinal, 39, 40
——— Count, 39; his connexion with the Dudley family, 40
Carrara, 72
Casale, surrender of, 52
——— Andrea, 22, 23
Catacombs, 121, 122
Cava (?), Cardinal, 57
Cesena, 87
Cesi, Cardinal, xxvi.
Chameleon, 129
Chamois, 136
Chapman, Alexander, xi.
Charles I. of England, 16, 19, 20, 55
——— II., 137, 138; his restoration unwelcome at Rome, 6; his expulsion from France, 55
Chesterfield, Earl of; see Stanhope.
Chigi; see Alexander VII.
——— Cardinal, 8
——— Don Mario, 9, 80
Chinese books, 135
Christina, Queen of Sweden, 67; her reception into the Roman Church, xii., xxi., 68-70
Cibò, Cardinal, 71, 72
Clement V., Pope, 50
——— IX.; see Rospigliosi.
——— X.; see Altieri.
Codex cited as a witness, 93
Colonna, Cardinal, 33, 34, 52
——— Carlo, 34
——— Constable, 33
——— family, 34, 51
Como, Lake of, 90, 91
Conclaves, account of, xxv., 139
Cooke, Alexander, xxviii., 140
Corradi, Cardinal, 80
Cosmo III. of Tuscany, travels of, 89
Costaguti, Cardinal, 59, 61
Couley, Timothy, 137
Cousi (?), 32

Crashaw, Richard, 37
Créqui, Duke of, 77, 80, 81
Cromwell, 54; portrait of at Florence, 89
Crystals, 123
Cupids with a vizard, 117

Desmarests, cards invented by, 127, 128
Dioscorides, translation of, xviii.
Donati, Giulio, 74
Donghi, Cardinal, 60, 62
Doué, 127
Dudley, Sir Robert, 40
Durazzo, Cardinal, 62

Eagle, Roman, 117
Elci, Cardinal de, 106, 107
Eminency, title of, 15
England, interference of Rome in, 17, 20, 55
Estampes-Valençay, Henri de, xxvi., 139
Este, Cardinal d', 55-59, 62
Etna, 123
Evelyn, John, xi., xxi.
Executions at Rome, 12, 13, 74
Eye, model of, 126

Pachenetti, Cardinal, 45, 46
Farnese, Cardinal, 107, 108
Filomarini, Cardinal, 41, 42
Florence, x. 89
Foppa, Mgr. 43
Fossils, 126, 127
Francietti, Cardinal, 63, 64

Gabrielli, Cardinal, 44, 15
Gaetani, family, 34
Gascoin, Sir Bernard, 89
Genoese, character of, 63
Gibbs, Dr. 23
Ginetto, Cardinal, 26-28
Giorio, Cardinal, 48
Giustiniani, Prince, 100
Gondi, Cardinal; see Retz
Gregory XI., Pope, 50
——— XV., 41, 43
Grimaldi, Cardinal, 46
Gualdo - Priorato, Count, 54, 78
Gualtieri, Cardinal, 102

Halifax, Lord; see Saville
Hall, mines of, 120
Harbledown, xiii.. xvii.
Harrach, Cardinal, 32, 33
Henrietta Maria, Queen of England, xviii., 11
Hercules, 116, 117
Hesse, Cardinal of, 98, 99
——— Landgraves of, 99
Holstenius, Lucas, 69
Homodei, Cardinal, 79, 80

Illustrissimo, title of Cardinals, 15
Imperiale, Cardinal, 80
Independents, Romanists disguised as, 20
Indian (American) curiosities, 136, 137
Inspruck, 69, 70
Innocent VIII., Pope, 71
——— IX., 45
——— X., 25, 36, 45, 51, 53, 71, 92, 100, 108, 118, &c.
——— XI.; see Odeschalchi
Inquisition as to books, 57, 58
Irish rebels, negotiations of Rome with, 17-19
Italians, the papacy confined to, 50

Jansen, Cornelius, xii., 132
Jansenists, 86
Jesuits, advice of to Alexander VII., 7; machinations of in England, 20; saying against them, 49; why not elected to the papacy, ib.
Juxon, Archbishop, xiii.

Key, ancient, 117
Kircher, Athanasius, 118, 134

La Blée, Madame, abbess at Lyons, 30-32
Lachrymatories, 122
Lancelotti, family, 44
Laud, Archbishop, 18-20, 55
Leda, 117
Leopold, Emperor, crowned as King of Bohemia, xii., 33

## INDEX.                                                   143

Leti, Gregorio, xxiii., xxiv.;
  his apology for the "Cardinalismo," 6
Loadstones, 119, 120
Lomellini, Cardinal, 80
Loretto, 37, 140
Louis XIII., King of France, 53
——— XIV., 128
Lucca, 64, 65; the "Volto Santo" of, 65
Ludovisi, Cardinal, 91, 92
——— Prince, 91, 92, 119
Lugo, Cardinal de, 49, 50
Lunsford, Sir Thomas, 140
Lyons, 30

Maculano, Cardinal, 42-44, 86
Maldacchini, Cardinal, 95-98
——— Donna Olympia, 36, 39, 66, 67, 81, 91, 95, 96, 100, 102, 103, 108, 109, &c.
Manchester, Earl of, xii.
Mantua, Duke of, 52
Maria, Sta., della Vittoria, 116
Masaniello, xi., 41
Mattei, Villa, 43
Mazzarini (Mazarin), Cardinal, 20, 25, 51-55, 76, 77, 128
——— junior, 52, 54
Medici, Carlo de', Cardinal, 10
——— Gior. Carlo de', Cardinal, 88, 89
——— See Tuscany, Cosmo III.
Melzi, Cardinal, 106
Mercury, 117
Metella, Cæcilia, tomb of, 118
Milan, 82, 83
Milton, John, 55
Modena, 57, 59
Monaco, transferred from Spanish to French garrison, 46
——— Prince of, ib.
Monte Real, Count of, Viceroy of Naples, 39
Morton, Albert, xviii., xix.

Navona, Piazza, 118
"Nipotismo di Roma," xxiv., xxvii.
Nonantola, 56
Nuns, gifts of, costly, 127

Obelisks, 73, 118, 119, 122
Odescalchi, Cardinal (Innocent XI.), 88-91
Olivares, 13, 14
Optical instruments, 131-135
Orsini, Cardinal, 50, 51
——— family, ib.
Osborne, Frances; see Bargrave.
Ottobuoni, Cardinal (Alexander VIII.), 103

Padrone, title of, 15
Palestrina, Prince of, 100
Pallavicino, Cardinal, 110, 111
Pall Mall, game of, 75
Palmer, Sir Henry, xviii.
Palotta, Cardinal, 34-37
Pamfili, Camillo, 95
——— Prince, 96
Pantheon, 16
Panzirollo, Cardinal, 11, 16, 66
Paolucci, Cardinal, 111
Parma, Duke of, 15, 21, &c.
Paske, Dr., xiii.
Paste antiche, 123
Paul V., Pope, 13
Pistols, pocket, forbidden at Rome, 12
Pio, Cardinal, 101, 102
Pluckley, xiii., xvii.
Plot, Dr., 122
Poison, antidote to, 127
Porcupine, 137
Prague, battle of the White Mountain, 116
Prassede, Sta., Abbot of, 43
Prayers for the dead, 122
Priests unpopular at Rome, 13
——— ancient Roman, 117
Proserpine, 117

Rafts, 118
Raggi, Cardinal, 92-95; story of his uncle, 93

Raymond, John, x., xix.-xxi.
——— Thomas, xix.
Reggio, 57
Reliques, 140
Retz, Cardinal de, xi., 76-78
Richard, St., King of Wessex, 65
Richelieu, Cardinal, 52, 53
Rinuccini, 20, 55
Rochelle, mussels of, 135
Romulus, 116
——— son of Maxentius, circus of, 118
Rondinini, Cardinal, 61
Rospigliosi, Cardinal (Clement IX.), 9, 68
Rossana, Princess of, 95
Rossetti, Cardinal, xxv., 16-20, 55
Rossi, J. J., engraver and publisher, xxii., 3, 5, 8, 138

Sacchetti, Cardinal, 24-26, 53
Salerno, 124
Sanderson, Bishop, xiii.
Sandoval, Cardinal de, 13, 14
Santa Croce, Cardinal, 83, 84
Sarpi, Paolo, 110
Savelli, Cardinal, 73-76
——— Duke, 5, 6
——— family, 74
Saville, Sir George (afterwards Lord Halifax), 74, 75
Savoy, Duchy of, 66
Selleck, Archdeacon, xv., xvi., 137, 138
Sforza, Cardinal, 72, 73
Shaban Aga, 137, 138
Sheldon, Archbishop, xiii.
Siena, x., xi., 58
Simplon, 123
Snake, figure of, 117
Solfaterra, 125
Spada, Cardinal Bernardino, 21-24, 60; his epigram on the death of Charles I., 24
——— Cardinal G. B., 84, 85

Stanhope, Philip Lord, afterwards Earl of Chesterfield, xi., xii., 11, 124
——— Lady, xi., 11
" Statera de' Porporati," xxiii.-xxv. ; Supplements to the " Statera," xxv., 139
Stefano, Sto. del Caco, 117
Stiletto, 136
Style, Roman, 127
Swan, Sir William, xi., 11, 12

Talarii Ludi, 117
Testana, Joseph, artist, 59, 61
Thomas Aquinas, 124

Tiber, figure of, 117
Tivoli, Confetti di, 125
Todd, Archdeacon, xxi.
Toulouse, mummies at, 130
Tuscany, Cardinal of ; see Medici, Carlo de'
——— Grand-Dukes of, 21, 25, 88, 89, 92

Urban VIII., Pope, 23, 24, 25, 28, 29, 32-36, 38, 41, 42, 44-46, &c. ; his nepotism, 14, 15; his war with the Princes of Italy, 10, 21, 39, 42, 45, 55, 74, 94, &c.

Vannuccio, Giuseppe, 9

Velletri, 28
Venetian lantern and stiletto, 136
Vesuvius, 123
Vidman, Cardinal, 75, 76
Virginian money, 140
Viterbo, 39

Westleius, optician, 134, 135
Wilde, Sir John, xvii.
Winchilsea, Lord, 123
Wotton, Sir Henry, xviii., xix., 123

York, Duchess of (Mary of Modena) 59

Zacchia, Cardinal, 61

---

Nichols and Sons, Printers, 25, Parliament Street, Westminster.

www.ingramcontent.com/pod-product-compliance
Lightning Source LLC
Chambersburg PA
CBHW020302170426
43202CB00008B/465